Democracy and Truth

Democracy and Truth

A Short History

Sophia Rosenfeld

PENN

UNIVERSITY OF PENNSYLVANIA PRESS

PHILADELPHIA

Published by
University of Pennsylvania Press
Philadelphia, Pennsylvania 19104-4112
www.upenn.edu/pennpress

Printed in the United States of America

Library of Congress Cataloging-in-Publication Control Number:
2018051029

ISBN 978-0-8122-5084-8 hardcover
ISBN 978-0-8122-9585-6 ebook

For Matthew

Contents

A Very Short Introduction   1

1. The Problem of Democratic Truth   4

2. Experts at the Helm   42

3. The Populist Reaction   92

4. Democracy in an Age of Lies   137

   Notes   177
   Acknowledgments   213

A Very Short Introduction

This book is intended as a short history in two senses. First, the whole amounts to only about two hundred pages. Second, the timeframe has been radically circumscribed; it covers not the entire story of democracy going back to the ancient world but rather its modern manifestation since the eighteenth century. The central premise is that a historically particular and even peculiar relationship between democracy and truth took root roughly two hundred fifty years ago on both sides of the Atlantic, and this relationship has shaped political life into the twenty-first century—in the United States and with important variations, in capitalist democracies around the globe. To understand the apparent crisis in truth today requires grappling with this history.

What this glance backward reveals, first and foremost, is that truth under the conditions of modern democracy has always been fragile. Truth—meaning doubly the opposite of lies (in moral terms) and the opposite of mistaken beliefs and erroneous information (in terms of epistemology)—has been touted as a key democratic value from the get-go. Republics and, later, modern democracies have long prided themselves on both building on

1

and generating truths in ways that constitute a striking departure from absolutist rule, whether in the mold of King Louis XIV or in the style of the modern dictator. That's why the seemingly brazen flourishing of misinformation and falsehoods in public life now can strike us as so shocking. And yet, democratic truth has never had any precise contours or content. Even if honesty, transparency, and factuality have, since the Enlightenment, been held in high regard as political values, truth has generally been understood not as dogma, but as the product of multiple constituencies in an inegalitarian world pursuing it according to varied methods and as continually open to fresh challenges and revision. No one can call all the shots. That means truth has also always been precarious, not to mention wrapped up in social strife along class, racial, religious, and educational lines. It has also been regularly subject to attempted hijackings—from above and from below, from the left and from the right—as different cohorts have worked hard to try to gain a monopoly on it. This book situates what is happening around us right now in this historical framework—a short one, indeed, but not so abbreviated and present-minded that we can't gain some necessary perspective.

Chapter 1 opens with an account of what pundits in the United States and elsewhere have, since 2016, increasingly been calling our "post-truth" present. It then considers the accuracy of this label from the vantage points of philosophy followed by history, focusing especially on the role of truth in the modern democratic imaginary that first blossomed in the Age of Revolutions and has survived, with important modifications, down to the present. Chapters 2 and 3 take up the greatest long-term threats to this idea: the rise of an elite, technocratic approach to the determination and propagation of truth and, then, a populist pushback—two phenomena that turn out to have surprising commonalities. Chapter 4, finally, asks what, if anything, has changed as of late to create a crisis in truth, paying special attention to some of the culprits favored by contemporary commentators, including the influence of postmodern theory, right-wing radio and television, and social media bubbles. The book concludes with the suggestion (if a historian can be indulged on this front) of some possible antidotes, large and small, and some thoughts on the truth/democracy relationship looking forward. Does democratic politics really "*need* truth to do its business well," as some have recently claimed?[1] If your hunch is yes, let's consider how you (and others) came to feel this way in the first place—and also why it still matters.

Chapter 1

The Problem of Democratic Truth

For the past few years, the mainstream press has repeatedly told us the same dark story. Democracy is in trouble in the United States—and the trouble extends to its very foundations. According to this narrative, citizens are losing their grip on any shared view of reality, the minimum requirement for the collective imagination and instantiation of a collective future.

The evidence appears to be everywhere. Think all the way back to Pizzagate, the bizarre, widely discussed 2016 story of an alleged child-sex ring being run by the Democratic Party out of the basement of a D.C. pizza joint. To this day, retellings—at least in the circles of the worried—inspire laughter, but also expressions of dismay. Laughter because, on the surface, the story is so preposterous. Dismay because, like many other such improbable, quasi-political hoaxes and conspiracy tales these days, it actually had its adherents, who can easily locate one another online. One believer even traveled to Washington, armed, looking to "self-investigate" on behalf of his aggrieved and mistrustful ideological compatriots. This is but the inverse of the hordes of school-shooting deniers who have been harassing teenagers in Parkland, Florida, convinced that the adolescent survivors of a 2018 high school mass murder aren't traumatized activists but rather "crisis actors," starring in an entirely faked piece of antigun propaganda. We now know that many of these Internet-fueled fairytales were concocted with the support of Russian intelligence forces and disseminated with the help of bots or "troll-factories" aiming to spread chaos in the run-up to the 2016 presidential election and beyond.[1] But others have been scams promulgated by obscure, for-profit companies right here in the United States or by popular websites like Gateway Pundit, which has relentlessly pushed "false flag" narratives.[2] They have also been helped along by giant, international web-based media platforms like YouTube and Facebook and search engines like Google looking, as always, for profits. Today's world of online news is full not just of partisan stories but also of false ones, designed to scare, anger, and mislead for political or mercenary ends.

It's not just a question of new media, though. Cable TV, talk radio, and even much of print journalism also relentlessly generate and push misleading stories or exaggerate the significance of real ones, often with the claim that they are supplying "balance." Spokespeople in Washington, from heads of advocacy groups to members of Congress, do the same. Fake audio and video may soon be so convincing that we will no longer be able to distinguish them from the real anyway.[3]

Then there is the current president himself, Donald Trump, widely considered both a symptom and an accelerant of our move away from any shared standards of truth. With his public pronouncements, whether on Twitter, at live rallies, or during visits to *Fox & Friends,* our former "reality TV"–star president has exacerbated the problem. He has also, with the support of a large cast of elected and unelected characters, added his own twists.

Trump, it is widely acknowledged, has always brazenly traded in misinformation. He makes up facts about his own past actions. He passes along tall tales from dubious sources. He denies the validity of legitimate information. And he keeps peddling these falsehoods even when they contradict his own or associates' previous claims. That goes for accusations and self-justifications alike. You've heard them all before: he's worth ten billion dollars; Muslims celebrated in New Jersey on 9/11; Obama isn't an American citizen; the tax cuts are going to hurt his rich friends and his own bottom line; there are terrorists from the Middle East hiding out in a caravan of Central American invaders; he never referred to "shithole" countries in Africa; climate change is a Chinese hoax; voter fraud is rampant; his personal health is magnificent; Democrats forced the breakup of families at the southern border because it's "their law"; he's been exonerated in the Mueller investigation; 3,000 people didn't die in a hurricane in Puerto Rico; and he doesn't know Stormy Daniels, except when he does. The list is long. The *Washington Post* says he made more than 2,000 false or misleading (as in the case of extremely exaggerated or selective) statements in his first 355 days in office, or about 5.6 per day.[4] The rate has increased substantially in year two of his presidency.[5]

But it is his response when shown legitimate proof to the contrary that draws our attention as much as the original lies. One of his favorite strategies when under fire is to suggest that all truth is slippery because it depends on whom one is talking to. Think of his predilection for statements beginning "Some people are saying . . . ," or "I've been hearing . . . ," or the comments delivered with a literal shrug or scare quotes suggesting "maybe" or "don't take my words so literally, it's all bullshit in the end." Other times he insists that he knows best, evidence be damned ("Believe me . . ."). Or he throws out totally bogus forms of corroboration (an especially cold New Year's Eve 2017 undermines claims of global warming; he might have audio recordings that would exonerate him from some act or other, though they never materialize) or implausible denials, as if it's all part of one big substance-free game. Most frequently, he insists the so-called "authorities" aren't actually authoritative at all, just more partisan players in a thoroughly political world. From the Congressional Budget Office to the Centers for Disease Control and Prevention to the *New York Times* and other "mainstream" or establishment information sources, it's "fake news" all the way down. In his telling, America's primary media are so corrupt that he's perfectly justified in lying to them.[6] In Trumpland, truth becomes falsehood, and falsehood masquerades as truth. The credibility of *any* source, indeed the very idea of verified knowledge itself, is thus thrown into question.

Some of this looseness with truth is intended as a form of distraction or a way to sow confusion, doubt, and maybe even fatigue in the public. Some is a power game, especially when subordinates and others currying favor, from official spokespersons to hacks on television, are forced to repeat the lies. Trump demonstrates just how much he can get away with and ensures his lackeys' loyalty along the way.[7] Some might even stem from reverse pride—specifically the fact that the president sees himself as capable of deciding from the gut (aided by a lot of cable-news watching) and does not need to rely on fancy-pants studies or the opinions of the so-called informed. In seeming to cut through the official bullshit, he is taking the establishment down a peg, at least rhetorically, and elevating himself, like a king, as the real source of truth. He is also, in the process, throwing off one more undesirable form of restraint. Cue up the photos of Trump looking straight at the eclipse in 2017 when everyone else has been warned by scientists not to do so. It is sometimes hard to tell with these gestures what is shrewd attention-grabbing combined with old-fashioned deceit and what is insecurity, impetuosity, or actual self-delusion, fulfilling his own fantasies of himself and the world.

Regardless of motivation, though, it is very clear that this antitruth stance goes beyond a stylistic choice; it has been translated into a mode of governance for the Trump administration as a whole. The same indifference to the boundaries between truth and falsehood, information and know-nothingism, has led to an actual turn away from the cultivation of institutional expertise in areas like macroeconomic policy, foreign affairs, and climate science. The gutting, in terms of both dollars and personnel, of the State Department, the Environmental Protection Agency, and many other government agencies, including fact-finding ones, constitutes a form of opposition to the research protocols and evidence-based knowledge that has long informed democratic procedures and policy in practice.[8] So does the elevation in their place of those who are, at all times, in the business of partisan pitching or selling, or what we might call political hacks, over experienced civil servants. Lying to cover up a culture of self-dealing—traditionally known in politics as corruption—seems to be another, closely related effect.

Yet what is perhaps most alarming, according to this narrative, is that many people in the United States and elsewhere appear not to care.[9] On the contrary, they seem to embrace this approach to the realm of truth and falsehood. More and more citizens are convinced, according to recent studies, that there are no such things these days as impartial, consensual facts. More and more citizens are also convinced that there are no legitimate, trustworthy sources of disinterested information, only partisan propaganda machines spinning out obfuscation, lies, and biased claims to advance hidden causes. This is increasingly the case on both sides, but particularly so, studies have found, on the right, and especially when it comes to institutions that promote shared norms of inquiry, including government agencies, universities, scientific research centers, media, and publishing companies.[10] In this context, what is important—indeed, what's actually believable and convincing as truth—is that what's stated *feels* authentic or conforms to a preexisting sentiment, not that it's accurate in some demonstrable way. "Truth" has become personal, a matter of subjective feeling and taste and not much different from an opinion (think "my truth").

Moreover, what counts as truth is now shaped to a substantial degree by group loyalty and partisanship—or what David Roberts, writing in *Vox*, calls "tribal epistemology."[11] We don't believe—which is to say, take to be true—that anyone on our team could do something illegal or say something deceptive, even when shown proof. That's because it doesn't fit our desired storyline. (Al Gore, referring to human-made environmental degradation, once called such information, cribbing from Max Weber, "inconvenient truth.")[12] But we might believe that crime by immigrants, say, or the incidence of violent crime in general is up because that's the way it seems in some impressionistic way—and also because it runs counter to the knowledge associated with our social and political enemies. This kind of confirmation bias is then reinforced in a media landscape in which we pick the news source that best matches our preexisting inclinations and affinities and dismiss the rest, à la Trump, as "garbage," "nonsense," or, most often, "fake news," meaning these days something we just don't want to hear. For like all successful slogans, the expression "fake news" has just enough truth to it—news reporting is, after all, often biased in different ways—to make it seem, if not accurate, then at least no more misleading than anything else.

Indeed, it is by this logic that Trump, with his blunt, knowledge-free, and often inaccurate pronouncements, can actually appear to a large segment of Americans to be *more* truthful than other politicians. In throwing over the social niceties and rejecting the euphemistic language of the educated establishment (otherwise known as "political correctness"), it looks to many people like he is actually telling it like it is, whether what he is saying is verifiable or not. Calling African countries "shitholes" may be unfounded and racist, but it is how "real" people think and talk in private. Trump is just brave enough to do so in public forums. Or so the thinking goes. Says presidential ally and long-time master of political dirty tricks Roger Stone, "Trump is a truth-teller. He calls it as he sees it. . . . To those who say this is divisive, well, we're tired of polite." As to the president's eschewing of evidence and accuracy, Stone's response is "How many angels can dance on the head of a pin? It's a question that can't be answered. Facts are, obviously, in the eye of the beholder. You have an obligation to make a compelling case. Caveat emptor."[13] This deliberate elevation of emotional frankness and the salesman's convincingness over veracity at a factual level also helps explain why, despite his history of outright prevarication about himself and the world, Trump was judged considerably more honest than his opponent, Hillary Clinton, right before the election that gave him the presidency.[14]

This all sounds peculiarly American perhaps—except the evidence suggests that it isn't happening only here. Disinformation has gone global, and not only because of the workings of Russian agents eager to benefit from the disruption of politics as usual. Hoaxes and conspiracy theories have fueled support for right-wing parties in many parts of Europe, especially when they depend on anti-immigrant sentiment. Consider how Viktor Orbán and his far right Fidesz party have cemented power in Hungary by pushing the phony notion that the European Union, the United Nations, and George Soros are together waging a battle to force the nation to accept thousands of mainly Muslim migrants and become an "immigrant country" rather than a white, Christian one.[15] Conversely, copycat charges of "fake news" on the part of quasi-authoritarian rulers all over the world looking to paper over corruption or to discredit unpleasant verities are now commonplace too. The leaders of Myanmar, including the Nobel Peace Prize–winning Aung San Suu Kyi, were, for example, quick to announce that there is "no such thing as the Rohingya," and it was all "fake news" on the part of outsiders when accused by the foreign press of flirting with the genocide of the country's Muslim minority this past year.[16] Different publics around the globe have, in imitation, embraced these strategies too. Everywhere, extreme partisan politics seems to be eating away at the truths held in common, by ordinary people as well as experts and representatives of the state, that a robust democratic public sphere ostensibly requires.

But has the "reality-based community," as a senior advisor to former President George W. Bush memorably dismissed those who remain wedded to a world of facts, actually become obsolete, a relic of a more naïve era? Are we really at the dawn of a brave new world of *post*-truth, to employ the 2016 *Oxford English Dictionary* word of the year, or an "epidemic of dishonesty," in the expression of former New York City mayor Michael Bloomberg?[17] And if so, is democracy (as we understand it today) doomed?

We can look at this question from several perspectives. Historians tend to be cynics. By their measure, there is rarely anything totally new under the sun. Truth and politics have, after all, never been on very good terms, and there has always been lying in politics, which depends at its core upon leaders skilled in the art of persuasion combined with a dose of hypocrisy for good measure. The ancients, starting with Plato and Aristotle, knew that well. An exceptional number of political leaders ever since, from kings to presidents and prime ministers, have provided us with shining examples across every kind of regime. The political theorist Hannah Arendt said it most famously in her great essay "Lying in Politics," in which she insisted that "deception, the deliberate falsehood and the outright lie used as legitimate means to achieve political ends, have been with us since the beginning of recorded history. Truthfulness has never been counted among the political virtues, and lies have always been regarded as justifiable tools in political dealings."[18]

Real "fake news," it turns out, is a very old phenomenon too. Pornographic *libelles* featuring a sex-obsessed Marie-Antoinette in the years before the French Revolution are simply the ancestors of today's "news stories" claiming Michelle Obama or Melania Trump is actually a man, or a body double, or a lesbian, or anything else salacious.[19] Conspiracies starring Jews have been a media staple from the Middle Ages to, well, the age of George Soros today.[20] Ditto for conspiracy theorists' suggestions that what appears to be reality is, in fact, staged in the service of mass persuasion.[21] In 1796, at the end of his presidency, in a passage that now sounds remarkably familiar, George Washington noted that during the previous few years the gazettes have "teemed with all the Invective that disappointment, ignorance of facts, and malicious falsehoods could invent, to misrepresent my politics and affections, to wound my reputation and feelings, and to weaken, if not entirely destroy, the confidence that you [the public] have been pleased to repose in me."[22] He wasn't wrong. Subsequent presidents have often felt equally victimized by an unscrupulous and biased press. It is the idea of objectivity in news reporting that is historically anomalous and a relatively recent invention. The aim of entirely disinterested judgment only began to characterize any of the truth-related professions in the wake of the rise of new scientific ideals in the middle of the nineteenth century.[23]

Moreover, it seems that many of us—despite this seemingly repetitive history—are always ready to declare ourselves seriously worried. In the modern world, concerned citizens and their journalistic spokespeople intermittently but serially go into moral panic mode in which they wring their collective hands about how to restore some imagined prior state of truthfulness that would make politics an altogether less unsavory and less manipulative business than it currently is. The late 1960s and early 1970s was one such moment, when Arendt wrote both "Lying in Politics" and "Truth and Politics," issuing an unusual defense of a limited purview for old-fashioned lying as essential to political action, alongside a discussion of the dangers of new forms of untruthfulness, like spin, that had emerged in the wake of the revelations of the *Pentagon Papers*.[24] (Interestingly, the *Pentagon Papers*—the secret "official" history of the Vietnam War that was leaked to the press at the height of that conflict and that exposed the gap between known facts and the pronouncements and decisions of the political class—are the subject, too, of the 2017 Steven Spielberg film *The Post,* which was calibrated to make an example of this same moment for our own times.) A similar public rhetoric of dismay kicked in all over again in the United States in the wake of the revelations of Watergate later that decade, the cover-ups of the Reagan presidency in the 1980s, and the Clinton impeachment debacle in the 1990s. Most recently, the falsehoods of the Bush administration, primarily the claims about weapons of mass destruction used to justify the invasion of Iraq in 2003, spawned a slew of new books with titles that screamed "deception," "hoax," "fraud," and "lies and the lying liars who tell them," as well as generated Merriam-Webster's 2006 word of the year, "truthiness."[25] Now, in the late 2010s, we have the closely related "post-truth" moment.[26]

However, before we decide if this time is different, we also need to consider the philosopher's answer to the question "Are we now post-truth?" A serious response requires something more than a simple yes or no. Namely, it depends on what is meant by truth. Questions about truth are rarely as clear-cut as one might wish, given that we are confronted immediately with problems of categorization, as well as issues related to both the production of knowledge and ethics.

Partly the answer to "Are we post-truth?" requires knowing what *kinds* of truths we are talking about. Do we mean mathematical or logical truths, like "2 plus 2 equals 4" or "My mother's mother is my grandmother"? Do we mean empirical truths or what Arendt called factual truths, which concern contingent events and are thus necessarily a posteriori ("Yesterday I bought my cereal at the Acme supermarket," or Arendt's own example, "On the night of August 4, 1914, German troops crossed the frontier of Belgium")?[27] Or do we mean eternal truths or normative, moral truths ("God is great" and "Lying is wrong"), where it is very hard to determine the boundaries among truth, belief, and opinion, and where exceptions are legion? What *are* truths in the political realm?

Even more, though, the answer depends upon what we accept as *means* or *standards* of validation and proof. There are, after all, also multiple ways of determining what counts as truth and takes on the status of legitimate knowledge, especially if we don't start from a position of dogmatic certainty. To make matters more complicated, these methods are often institution- or discipline-specific.

15

Different approaches depend on different kinds of social foundations too.

Some basic ways of discovering and verifying truth begin and end with the individual. They are derived from personal experience, meaning largely evidence derived from one's senses. Or they depend on the exercise of logic and inference from prior experiential knowledge. They can, in some instances, even stem from faith or gut instinct. But most important truths come to light or are confirmed and conveyed as legitimate, reliable knowledge only as a result of communication with those around us—that is, via active discussion or consultation based on comparing or combining one's experience or hunches or rational guesses and hypotheses with those of others. We necessarily learn most truths from other people and, as Socrates noted a very long time ago, in the public sphere.

And that's not all. Often the acquisition of full or even partial knowledge also requires trust in authorities at a distance, unknown to us except by reputation, institutional affiliation, or some other form of external validation. In such instances, we have to defer, in part or in whole, to those to whom we've granted the title "experts" in the domain in question. That can mean those who generate and certify knowledge in the first place, like scientists, economists, historians, or specialists in government agencies such as the Congressional Research Office or the Bureau of Labor Statistics, all of whom employ different standards of data collecting, evidence, modeling, and testing depending on field and context. It can also mean the legitimate media, from "mainstream" newspapers to TV stations to university and commercial presses, which have been tasked with reporting and explaining such findings to laypeople or even those with specialized knowledge in different domains. That is because it is impossible for anyone to have the capacity or prior knowledge to weigh and determine the veracity of every claim in question on his or her own. We can't easily know what we haven't observed—that it was 90 degrees Fahrenheit in the Malian city of Ségou on August 10, 1995. That's the kind of information that needs to be looked up. And even in cases in which we do have some personal experience—it was 90 degrees Fahrenheit in my house in Philadelphia this past weekend—we can't easily know what causes what. There is simply too much to know. So much of that knowledge, both what it is and how it was obtained, is difficult to comprehend too, not least when it comes to the myriad concerns of modern political life. Trust in others becomes imperative.

Furthermore, no matter which of these modes of knowledge-acquisition and knowledge-sharing we are talking about, truth and truthfulness do not always occupy the same page either, since the one refers more to accuracy and the other to authenticity and moral virtue. Lying generally covers only those instances involving deliberate untruths; lies are ethical lapses that speak to character. However, one can sincerely and candidly convey what turns out to be a falsehood or simply incorrect, as the Pizzagate believers demonstrate. One can also spew a truth without intending to do so, as arguably sometimes happens with President Trump, who doesn't always seem to be in full control of his words. The political consequences are undoubtedly different too, even if we generally agree that democracy in practice requires some fairly limited set of combined moral-epistemic convictions: that most people are telling the truth most of the time; that truth is distinct from falsehood; and that, in the end, we *can* tell the difference and that difference matters.[28]

So where do these philosophical conundrums leave us in terms of thinking about today? We can start by recognizing that dismay over our failure to find common ground in our conception of reality is, at present, primarily focused on empirical or factual truths (which are precisely the ones that Arendt warned us back in the 1970s have the most to do with politics) rather than moral or logical ones.

We have largely abandoned the idea that ready consensus about ethical or eternal truth, aside from a few platitudes, is necessary or even possible in a pluralist world. That is one reason religious belief has, in many democracies, been legally sequestered in the private sphere and rendered a matter of individual conscience. Many people do, of course, bring their private convictions into their public lives, and they often become points of contention in practice; but we do not generally expect that religious truths or teachings *should* be a source of ready agreement. Logical truth, meanwhile, lends itself in principle less often to dispute, though certainly the rational conclusions of the scientific establishment are increasingly subject to challenge today too, and we are also well aware that numbers, like words or images, can be manipulated to prove a variety of points. As Voltaire famously quipped, "there are no sects in geometry."

But empirical, factual truths are a different beast. They naturally and almost routinely prompt fights and generate denials, distortions, and inventions even as they are supposed to be beyond challenge. In part this is because of their insecurity; empirical facts are always ultimately dependent on others in the role of witnesses because they can't be shored up by reason alone. In part it's because even when we agree at a minimal level about what has happened, we often disagree about which claims deserve priority or how best to put them into words or figures. As statements about the world, they are rarely really neutral (think, for example, of all that is implied about the nature of work, age, and effort in an otherwise unadorned unemployment figure). Mainly it's because even the barest facts require interpretation, or assessments of their implications in light of other ideas or values, religious and not, in ways that quickly move us to the realm of opinion and hence both pluralism and conflict. There may be a single correct answer to "Does North Korea have nuclear weapons?" but there is no single right answer to "Is their existence a danger and to whom?" Even the seemingly unremarkable statement of fact that "The Civil War was fought over slavery" counts as a contested political claim in the United States today. Moreover, when we occasionally manage to agree on their content and meaning, empirical truths like this one never tell us what to do next.

At its heart, though, the current crisis belongs primarily to the realm of epistemology or *how* we know what we know. The fundamental issue for politics is ultimately not the moral question "Why is it important to be truthful?" But neither is it the ontological question "What is objective truth?" or even "What are facts?" Most philosophers today agree that there is some real world out there somewhere that exists independent of us or our languages for naming them.[29] Rather, the question is how can we best capture that reality and distinguish reliable knowledge about it from falsehoods, errors, bullshit, or even just unproven

19

belief. Which means that what is at stake is primarily whom we should entrust with the job of drawing these lines and how they should do it. Post-truth is, at heart, a struggle over *people* as holders of epistemic authority and over their different *methods* of inquiry and proof in an intensely partisan era.

Abstract as all of that sounds, here is where history does become useful, and historians have more to add than "it's always been thus." Epistemology may seem far removed from the rough and tumble of lived politics. But one doesn't have to have plunged fully into the waters of postmodernist relativism (which, despite many recent pundits' claims, has actually had little direct impact outside the academy and the arts) to accept two key historical points.[30] One is that, despite some seeming continuities, questions about how best to capture reality get answered differently at different junctures in history. We now know that paths, as well as obstacles, to producing, identifying, certifying, naming, and conveying truth actually vary over space and time and even by social group or individual within the same society. So do the nature of the fears of truth's absence or demise. The second, related point is that truth and its opposites are always implicated in questions of power—and thus truth is never fully divorced from politics or social conflict.

It was the French philosopher Michel Foucault who famously introduced us to the idea that different societies are governed by distinct "regime[s] of truth" or "'general politics' of truth." By this he meant different societies invested different kinds of people with the status and authority to determine what counts as truth and promoted different discourses, disciplines, means, and strategies for getting there (though he had very little to say about internal divisions within societies).[31] Historians of science, law, and other scholarly practices too have made us aware that even categories like "fact" and "evidence," so essential to the modern laboratory, the courtroom, and the nonfiction book or periodical, are not timeless constructs. They have a history of changing meaning and use that is inextricably linked with social, political, and economic life.[32] Lies and errors do as well.[33]

To take one example, in an influential 1994 study called *A Social History of Truth,* the historian of science Steven Shapin trumpeted the then-disconcerting idea that, at the height of the Scientific Revolution in seventeenth-century England, truth-telling had distinctive sociological parameters: it was understood to be the attribute of a particular social type, the independent gentleman. As a consequence, what the new science of the era took to be credible or trustworthy knowledge was not a universal standard but actually closely linked to an elite culture of honor, wealth, and proper, civilized comportment.[34] Another leading historian of science, Lorraine Daston, has similarly demonstrated how, during the following century, the empirical fact, derived originally from the direct experience of this disinterested gentleman, then came to be invested with a novel kind of certainty that gave it social utility. The fact became helpful both in halting conflicts and in bolstering what counted as true knowledge about an ever-increasing number of phenomena, including natural events and human actions alike.[35]

We should not be surprised, therefore, that modern democracy has a distinctive relationship to truth, knowledge, and its ostensible bearers. Neither should we be

surprised that this relationship is also a historical arti-
fact, albeit one with which we've now lived in the United
States for a few hundred years, so we may not actively
experience it as historical anymore. What we call democratic governance—a form of representative politics
that was known as republicanism at the outset and that
combines the protection of civil rights with popular sovereignty—owes much to the particular truth culture of
the transatlantic Enlightenment from which it emerged
in the second half of the eighteenth century.

What is essential to recognize for our purposes is that
the eradication of error and falsehood in the pursuit of
truth was the principal preoccupation around which the
European and colonial Enlightenment that followed the
Scientific Revolution revolved. At its core lay a deep antip-
athy to old habits and modes of thought, which *philosophes*
like Voltaire and Kant took to be, if not lies, then supersti-
tions, prejudices, and dogmas, or beliefs unmoored from
reason and evidence. The goal became not just to cultivate new methods for bringing real, verifiable truth or
knowledge into view. As a starting point, the Enlightenment entailed a closely related moral crusade against the
deceptive institutions, social norms, and language games
that, the *philosophes* believed, had long helped perpetuate
the realm of falsehoods and myths with deleterious effects
upon people everywhere.

Targets were plentiful. The Catholic Church got
branded an especial source of phony truths and misleading teachings—in ostensibly Catholic France as well as in
the Protestant British orbit. The infamous "philosophical
dictionaries" penned by Voltaire and the Baron d'Holbach
in the mid-eighteenth century are best described as efforts

to expose the hypocrisy behind the very words that made up Catholic doctrine, from faith or *foi* ("believing not what seems true, but what seems false to our understanding") to truth or *vérité* itself (what Jesus might have called "an abstract word which most men use indifferently in their books and judgments, for error and falsehood").[36] The manners and mores of aristocrats and other social elites, with their elaborate codes of etiquette, came in for similar attacks for perpetuating subterfuge and disguise, traits that were increasingly linked with effeminacy as well. And in the course of the eighteenth century, monarchies and courts themselves got reframed by critics on both sides of the Atlantic as places of secrecy and deceit, rife with intrigue, plotting, and various forms of "feminine" dissimulation designed to keep subjects and sometimes even the government's own ministers literally in the dark. Well before 1750, for example, the editors of the great early eighteenth-century English paper *The Craftsman* promised nothing less than to expose to its readers the *Craft*, or "Frauds, Abuses, and secret Iniquities," characteristic of modern *State-Craft*.[37]

All of this was new. From the days of Machiavelli to the courts of enlightened despots, good rulership had long been positively associated, if not exactly with blatant lying, then with shielding most state information and decision-making from the eyes and ears of the population at large and with dissimulation when necessary. Frederick the Great of Prussia could sensibly declare that one reason a private person couldn't legitimately offer his judgments about affairs of state was that, by definition, "he lacks complete knowledge of circumstances," and he wasn't about to get any.[38] (An essay contest that Frederick sponsored at the Academy of Berlin in 1780 on whether it was "useful to deceive the people" generated mixed responses.) Conversely, most kings saw little reason to look to public opinion to inform their own choices, as the public did not need to be appeased. However, in the later eighteenth century, past virtue turned into vice, at least for many of those steeped in the world of enlightened critique. One of the core sins of kingship became the way it thwarted communication between ruler and ruled. As Thomas Paine put it in characteristically cutting fashion, "There is something exceedingly ridiculous in the composition of monarchy; it first excludes a man from the means of information, yet empowers him to act in cases where the highest judgment is required . . . wherefore the different parts, unnaturally opposing and destroying each other, prove the whole character to be absurd and useless."[39]

Enter the republic. For eighteenth-century champions like Jean-Jacques Rousseau, the Abbé Mably, and indeed Thomas Paine, republics promised to put into play a diametrically opposed set of moral-epistemic values: transparency and openness; trust in others; and an ethos of truth-seeking and truth-telling at every level. Liberty and equality would go hand in hand with a commitment to demonstrable evidence and accuracy (rather than secrecy, lies, and errors) *and* a premium on sincerity and candor (over hypocrisy and corruption). That would be true of citizens and elected officials alike. In the spirit of "publicity," laws and other key political texts would be printed and distributed for all to read or hear or discuss. Meetings of new representative bodies would be open to spectators and auditors alike. Even ordinary people, going about their daily routines, would take off their figurative masks and become readable and thus accountable to one another in new ways. And what they would reveal would be their authentic selves, in Rousseau's telling. When the writer Louis-Sebastien Mercier tried, in the early 1770s, to imagine the world of the future, his Rousseau-inspired fantasy involved the whole society turning into a legible "book of morals," a true ethical and intellectual paradise, as well as a place where any residual instances of insincerity or lying would be subject to public censure.[40]

In the new United States, a legacy of Puritan investment in similar values—namely, the alignment of seeing and being, utterances and actions—only bolstered this Enlightenment vision, and vice versa, while also generating further suspicions of baroque, Catholic ways.[41] American Protestantism has continued (at least until the Trump moment) to reaffirm the value of believers' personal sincerity, of embodying a commitment to truth as opposed to deception or falsity in every aspect of life, not least in politics. Arendt saw this new "zeal for truthfulness," born originally of Protestant engagement with the New Testament together with the new science, to be one of the distinctive hallmarks of modernity.[42] And at the same time, a burgeoning capitalist marketplace on both sides of the Atlantic grew up dependent on related practices of interpersonal trust.

The modern republican imaginary took shape in the Age of Revolutions at the intersection of all of these trends. In the case of truth and what would eventually come to be called democratic governance, the promise was that one would become an instrument of the other. A moral and epistemic commitment to truth would undergird the establishment of the new political order; preexisting knowledge would be harnessed for public purposes. But participation in the political process would also, in the end, aid the cause of truth's discovery and expression.[43] Republics would make the (secular and Christian) Enlightenment dream of the coincidence of virtue and knowledge—or truth-telling in both senses—a reality.

But where would all this new, authoritative knowledge come from in this ideal arrangement? How would citizens of a republic actually know what was true? Herein lay the crux of the matter. Because, from their foundings, one of the key characteristics of republics or modern representative democracies—at least in theory—has also been a commitment to an undogmatic, open-ended conception of truth. Yes, governments premised on the idea of self-rule typically depend on the idea that the people should not be deceived, that veracity and authenticity matter as moral qualities for all. Nevertheless, they also generally insist that knowledge of the world—that which we collectively take to be true about the reality that surrounds us—continues to evolve and thus must always be subject to question, challenge, and potential revision. Nothing should be set in stone.

From this core principle, it also follows that no individual, sector, or institution can hold a monopoly at any point on determining what counts as truth in public life. Certainly, there can be no single source for knowledge of the divine. Republicanism went hand in hand with respect for a considerable amount of religious liberty in both the eighteenth-century French and North American contexts, though that would not always hold true as the republican model spread in the nineteenth and twentieth centuries, especially within Latin America.[44] But it is not just when things turn religious that this principle applies. In a republic as opposed to an absolutist or autocratic state, *worldly* truth—like power in general—has no exclusive or definitive source in public life either. Or to put it the other way, pluralism, along with a dose of skepticism inherited from the ancients, has, in theory, been a key characteristic of modern experiments with popular rule from the start. In part this was intended as a check on hubris (we are all, individually and collectively, fallible after all), and in part this was understood to be a way to maintain the peace when differences of judgment, whether about values, policies, or even facts, were inevitable. (Ideally, even those who derived their truths from revelation would have incentive to accept a pluralist conception of the public sphere since it gave them the space and liberty to hold nonliberal views.)[45] Despite claims here and there in the eighteenth century about the "self-evidence" of certain notions, truth in public life was generally thought of as something achieved or won in a social world, not a given starting point. As Arendt points out, when Thomas Jefferson added a "we hold" before the most celebrated such statement in the Declaration of Independence, he was subtly pointing out that even these truths were ultimately products of human agreement.[46]

The best, then, that could be imagined by the inventors of modern democracy was a division of labor on the epistemological front. For early European and North American advocates of republics even before they morphed into democracies, dependable knowledge, or truths by which to craft a life in common, had two major wellsprings. Both of them were human; both of them were communal; and both of them, together, were critical to effective governance in the context of self-rule.

One was the wisdom of the crowd, meaning the collective intelligence of the mass of ordinary, non–office-holding (though, it was assumed, white, male, and propertied) people, or what the French originally called in 1789 "active" citizens. Armed only with their own lived experience, the basic tenets of common sense and reason that were the common possession of "everyone" (generally defined as above, but contested from the start), and, a bit later, some basic education, they could be counted on to know something fundamental about not just their personal interests but also the common good. The second source of real knowledge in a republic was more rarified, if still similarly collective: the judgments of a special, albeit nebulous elite made up of the exceptionally educated, credentialed, and trustworthy. That group included those chosen as representatives (who initially required greater qualifications than the mass of voters and typically have been richer and more educated than their constituents to this day). Soon thereafter, it also involved those trained, via book learning and job experience, in the business of offering advice and counsel inside and outside the halls of government, or what would become today's unelected policy wonks, consultants, advisors, civil servants, and "deep state" actors.

The enduring idea is that the two sectors—ordinary people and the exceptionally virtuous, wise, and learned— would work in tandem, albeit with different roles to play. As Jefferson famously explained in the early days of the new United States, what a politics dedicated to the common good required was the "diffusion of knowledge" from above into "the hands of their [the people's] own common sense."[47] Not much has changed in this basic theoretical formulation since, even as the Progressives gave it new teeth starting in the 1890s. In working out the principles of justice, John Rawls declared almost two hundred years after the Declaration of Independence, "We must rely upon current knowledge as recognized by common sense *and* the existing scientific consensus," or the wisdom of the people together with the wisdom of elites (though Rawls, the great philosopher of liberalism, preferred to speak of "public reason" rather than of any kind of truth as the result).[48] We might even say that what would characterize democratic truth practices in their modern, post-1776 incarnation was less any particular institutional form than an abstract idea: of rational disagreement, or agonism, leading to a kind of symbiosis between these different social bodies and their different but complementary ways of knowing. Together they would generate a loose consensus, always precarious, always subject to reconsideration and adjustment, but the closest to a set of shared convictions or useful facts that we might hope to achieve as a platform for crafting government policy and for binding us all together in some minimal way. Today, the end result of this process is sometimes called "public knowledge" or, slightly more cynically, "serviceable truth" or "political truth."[49]

Still, how was it all intended to work? By what means was this epistemic ideal supposed to be realized? Let's look a bit more closely. At the heart of the modern republican idea, as developed in the Age of Revolutions that stretched from the late eighteenth into the middle of the nineteenth centuries, was the subsidiary idea that "ordinary" people, as the source of sovereignty, should be empowered, first, to share divergent views with one another and then to decide, via voting, on the broad outlines of a collective course of action or, at a minimum, on those who best represent their vision of a course of action. They would do so, in this vision, by employing a combination of basic empirical, logical, and normative moral truths, as well as personally held beliefs and values. Yet, it was also widely assumed from the start that ordinary people, even when restricted to those who were property-holding, male, and white, could not know everything necessary to make good decisions about the public good on their own, relying only on their local, partial knowledge. They required high-quality and broad-ranging information—about how things are, how they have been, and even how they might be—before they could ever decide what best to do going forward. That—or risk what contemporary philosopher Harry Frankfurt imagines as the pitiable condition of "having nothing to guide us but our own feckless speculations or fantasies and the importunate and unreliable advice of others."[50]

Thus ordinary people had to turn to some combination of elected officials and what would eventually be called "experts" to supply, candidly and transparently, the preliminary factual truths that they needed to make well-reasoned judgments at the ballot box about the larger natural world in which they lived, about the social and economic world they had constructed, even about how government works and the options before it. They would also require experts to filter out from ordinary discussions what is plain wrong, whether because it is mistaken or because it is a lie. All of this knowledge would be put to use by citizens in the crafting of opinions, in their public deliberations with others, and in their final votes.

Once the citizenry issued its conclusions (whether through consensus or the aggregation of divergent opinions), it would, however, again be up to experts, albeit often different ones working with elected officials, to hear those voters, or the people more broadly, and to try to figure out how best to implement their will or sense of the world. That was the expectation until that moment when nonexpert judgment would be required anew to determine the success of this latest strategy. And so it was supposed to go, back and forth, with something like pragmatic or political truth, rooted in some combination of knowledge, values, and beliefs, as the result.

Of course, much depended (and still does), de facto, upon trust in one's compatriots, known and not. Just as ordinary citizens have to have confidence in experts as well as one another to a considerable degree, believing these authorities to be honestly conveying the most accurate and objective information they have available, experts need to show themselves to be responsive to public feedback, abiding by popular mandates and subjecting themselves to scrutiny, for the whole system to work. Furthermore, elected political leaders have to be perceived as committed to telling the truth about what they know (though they can keep some things quiet). They also have to be understood as passing along to their constituents only information from verified sources. Otherwise they break the faith on which all of this runs. A late eighteenth-century French and American obsession with the swearing of oaths, or the promising of one's honesty as well as loyalty in various aspects of public life, suggests the deep interest early republicans had in making this trust a sure thing.

Yet the idea was never that trust or even oaths would alone suffice. It was also widely acknowledged that the pursuit of truth under the conditions of popular sovereignty depended on the cultivation of certain very specific habits, laws, and institutions, all concerned centrally with the process of communication. Shaping how people talked to one another promised to be the other key.

Plain speech, or a simple, anti-rhetorical style of address, was, for early theorists, the mode of communication required to make this whole trust and truth business run. Democracy, more than other forms of rule, turned on persuasion. But from Benjamin Franklin's Poor Richard alter ego of almanac fame to Jacobin civic catechisms, the goal of committed republicans became fostering the least showy and ostentatious language possible to make one's case. Virtue required a plain, unadorned style, which became a mark of one's honesty and candor. Epistemic clarity did as well, based on the post-Lockean idea that words necessarily mediated between people and ideas, but that truth must be allowed to speak for itself with as little interference on their part as possible. The ideal was a language in which the correspondence between signs and reality came as close to exact as could be. That way individuals could make themselves understood without risk of ambiguity, misunderstanding, or arousing suspicion about ulterior motives—and by those from all walks of life.[51] Plain speech would make meaningful and transparent dialogue possible across economic, educational, regional, and ideological divides.

Free speech, likewise, was deemed the essential legal principle for upholding this mode of rule. Hence the centrality of the articulation of speech rights along with voting rights in the Declaration of the Rights of Man in France and the early state constitutions, followed by the Bill of Rights, in the United States. From John Milton well before the Age of Revolutions to John Stuart Mill well afterward, consequentialists long justified a largely unrestricted realm of expression, just as much as a simple, transparent language in which to communicate, as a spur to the pursuit of truth. The idea was that competition— among ideas, thinkers, texts—would, in a world in which it was hard to be certain, ultimately work to dispel errors in fact and interpretation alike and to advance real knowledge, especially when it came to religious or philosophical claims. Truth would always be more persuasive than falsehood in the end. But with the advent of republics came the subsidiary idea that a largely free space for the exchange of ideas, including heterodox and critical ones, would do wonders to advance the particular (and particularly contentious) kinds of truths related to exercising the sovereignty of the people.[52] In fact, republics couldn't survive without it.

As early as the 1720s, the young Benjamin Franklin was quoting British sources in linking free speech to political freedom—"Without Freedom of Thought, there can be no such Thing as Wisdom, and no such thing as publick Liberty, without Freedom of Speech"—calling it a "sacred Privilege . . . essential to Free Governments."[53] By the last quarter of the eighteenth century, in North America and in France alike, it was widely argued that to fulfill their role as citizens, "the people" needed freedom of inquiry and expression for multiple practical purposes related to the process of arriving at public knowledge. First, in a world defined by popular sovereignty, all citizens had to have the ability to hear—which is to say, receive—all information and arguments relevant to their deliberations, including about the performance of the government, past and future. This particular form of freedom, first put into practice by the members of the Swedish Diet in 1766, was conceived as vital both to preventing tyranny (since even ostensibly honest governments always had reasons to try to cover up illegal or incompetent behavior) and to empowering citizens in the business of forming public opinion. Second, as legal scholar Alexander Meiklejohn tried to theorize in the middle of the twentieth century through drawing on the precedent of the colonial New England town meeting, all citizens had to have the ability, as part of democratic decision-making, to speak themselves and to share their own knowledge *and* beliefs. That way they would be able to increase the pool of possible ideas and challenge the dogmas of others, especially in areas in which agreement was hard to come by.[54] What's more, those same citizens had to be able to communicate those determinations back to the government and call out public servants when they did lie or mislead or otherwise run afoul of their constituents. This was the only way to truth. Such faith in the epistemic and moral value of unfettered debate is what kept James Madison convinced at the height of conflict over the parameters of free speech in the early 1790s that, in the end, "in a Republic, light will prevail over darkness, truth over error."[55] The risk of generating temporary strife or giving publicity to the occasional error, falsehood, or invective seemed a small price to pay for an openness that has now come to be seen as an essential feature of self-rule.

Indeed, it is not surprising that Franklin made his early version of this case for the necessary link between intellectual and political freedom in one newspaper (the *New England Courant*), citing another (the *London Journal*). Institutions associated with speech and communication, many of them independent of the state, had a mediating role to play in this process from the start. In particular, the commercial press, in all of the first republics to emerge from the Age of Revolutions, was understood to have a special job. That was assuming responsibility for not only conveying accurate, contextualized information to citizens to aid them in their deliberations but also, in what would come to be the investigative reporting tradition in the late nineteenth and early twentieth centuries, helping the people hold government officials accountable by checking their misstatements and fabrications, revealing their characters, and exposing what really happened behind closed doors. In addition, the press opened its pages early on to citizen comment and debate, becoming, potentially, both a forum for dissent from the mainstream of (generally elite) public opinion and a way to influence government. In 1774, the Continental Congress had already attributed to the press, "besides the advancement of truth, science, morality, and arts in general, in its diffusion of liberal sentiments on the administration of Government, its ready communication of thoughts between subjects, and its promotion of union among them," an essential public function.[56]

All those purposes only grew once republics were up and running. So did the kinds of institutions associated with fostering standards of truth. Courts of law played another critical role from the start in establishing and maintaining the truth practices associated with democracy. In the course of the nineteenth century, schools and universities, voluntary associations and learned societies, political parties, even the post office would all assist with this job, some from the inside and some at what was perceived to be a necessary distance from the state. The production and dissemination of undogmatic but usable, communal truth was to be aided by particular social cohorts, dispositions, processes, languages, laws, and institutions, all specific to democratic life.

Yet there is one major problem with this account. It was never more than a rough ideal or set of ambitions, whether in the hands of the authors of the *Federalist Papers* writing in an effort to secure the passage of the Constitution in the late 1780s, or John Dewey in the 1920s and 1930s, or advocates of deliberative democracy now. Certainly it bears little resemblance to how things *actually* were. At issue are not only all the specific structural or logical obstacles to the realization of this political vision—for example, that the press, as an instrument of politics and a product of market segmentation too, has long had good incentives to fill its pages with lies and partisan attacks just as much as with truths and certified knowledge, or that governments, by definition, cannot be truly transparent without giving up all their authority, or even that truth in politics is always more equivocal and fraught than one might like in part because many of us are often talking without sufficient knowledge to back up our claims. More significantly, in practice, history has transpired very, very differently.

Nothing like democracy, even in its representative form, has—quite obviously—ever actually been realized, even as the term ceased to be a pejorative in the early nineteenth century and instead became a label for a desirable, modern political arrangement. The public on which the idea rests was constituted, by definition, out of glaring exclusions, racial, gendered, and other, and many of these persist to this day in modified forms.[57] Vast inequality—of resources, education, and status alike—remains the norm as well.

Furthermore, nothing like the fully collaborative, trusting, enlightened "regime of truth" that I have described above has ever really come to pass, especially as it has become complicated by the values of commercial advertising followed by new forms of political partisanship, a vastly expanded public, and the flourishing, at intervals, of rival conceptions of political truth. At different historical moments, particular nations have moved closer to and further from this original model in terms of their experience, just as some leaders have done better than others as truth-tellers. But the exercise of democratic politics, including the specifics of its relationship to truth and knowledge, has remained an arena of struggle since the Founding moment, in the United States and elsewhere too. In fact, fights about the way to truth, sociologically and methodologically, may be as central to republican governance as fights about sovereignty and representation. Familiar conflicts over the nature and cost of education (including its secular and religious dimensions), or over the standards and responsibilities of the press, or over the meaning and parameters of freedom of speech, have often simply been proxies for this larger and ongoing struggle: over who *really* gets, and by what means, to say what is correct and true and over where the power attached to this prerogative is ultimately going to reside.

More specifically, the history of modern democracy, in the United States and in many other parts of the world, including much of Europe and Latin America, has been riven with a constant tension between the rule of expert truth, on the one hand, and the rule of majority instincts, on the other.[58] Both have had and have their legitimate roles to play. But too much of either in isolation—elite knowledge or popular consensus, without the corrective of the other—constitutes a danger to the whole edifice. Of course, those rules or norms of ostensible cooperation also help prop up the status quo in all its unfairness. That's what critics on both the left and right will say, and not without justification. The alternative, however, may well be worse.

There are those who, even today, build on a long tradition of extolling the superior wisdom and knowledge of the highly educated, especially when juxtaposed with the supposed ignorance and irrationality of ordinary people.[59] The idea, which goes back to the Founding, is that we would be best off empowering a true meritocracy, indeed an "epistocracy," even if it means instituting some limits on democracy. Especially as the world has grown so complex, it is silly to think that voters will not easily go, or be led, intellectually astray. Moreover, progress in many domains, such as global healthcare, has often come about in the contemporary world precisely when decisions have not had to go through democratic channels. But cognitive or scientific elites, rather than always knowing best, can—with too much power—become severely compromised as political actors, as chapter 2 will show. They can become blinded by their own credentials or motivated by self-interest (in short, money and power) and end up presenting the public with faulty or partial knowledge. They can also dangerously narrow the sphere of debate or decision-making by offering a narrow set of options. At an extreme, they can render real popular decision-making largely obsolete and then ignore the needs of the people whom they are supposed to have in mind, essentially removing them from the picture. Then we end up with full-scale technocracy, which is what many people see the modern "planning" state, from Washington to Brussels, as having become.

Yet invocation of the untampered rule of the people's common sense or populism—which seems to be having a moment of global resurgence in the 2010s—has its own obvious dangers, which will be explored in chapter 3. This is not to say that popular rule is inherently a problem from the perspective of ascertaining truth; there are good arguments sometimes made today, especially by so-called epistemic democrats, to the effect that "the people," when diverse in makeup, actually *do* know better.[60] Ever since the eighteenth century, the intellectual capacity of ordinary people has, as an idea, also helped fuel a variety of vital social movements. However, frequent dependence on conspiracy thinking regarding the nefarious ways of elite sources of epistemic authority, combined with a common attachment to instinct and candor over complexity and accuracy, easily deteriorates into a disdain for all forms of established knowledge and its purveyors, a central feature of the phenomenon of "post-truth." Then we end up not only with faulty and often simplistic policy proposals or checks on the variety of points of view and pluralism that are essential to successful democratic governance. We also create a fertile breeding ground for demagoguery. Plutocrats, after all, often make good populists.

Ironically, it is Maximilien Robespierre, who did so much to craft the tenets of modern democracy along with those of the modern police state, who saw the risk from both sides: "Democracy perishes by two excesses, the aristocracy of those who govern, or the contempt of the people for the authorities which it has itself established, a contempt in which each faction or individual reaches out for the public power, and reduces the people, through the resulting chaos, to nullity, or the power of a single man."[61] Champions of liberal versions of representative democratic governance have been trying to ward off both tendencies in their extreme form as real, and oddly parallel, dangers ever since.

We may not (yet) have reached a point of no return when it comes to post-truth. The phrase itself has already become partisan, much like "fake news," which Trump (fallaciously) now claims he invented.[62] But we do seem to be in a period of particular turmoil in which a resurgent populism in certain sectors is on a long-term collision course with many decades, if not centuries, of efforts to shore up policy-making based on technical knowledge designed by and for elites, with division rather than compromise the goal among their respective partisans. (This may also be one way that longstanding class-based and racial conflict get expressed in the twenty-first century.)

Also, as the final chapter demonstrates, we cannot ignore the trends that have severely exacerbated this situation in the very recent past. This encompasses a technological shift in information dissemination as massive as that which gave us mechanical printing in the fifteenth century. It also includes the advent of a twenty-four–hour news and entertainment cycle in which demand is constant, and juicy information, right or wrong, is instantly amplified by social media, with its tendencies toward exhibitionist vitriol on the one hand, and self-protective bubbles of like-mindedness on the other. Equally, if not more important, has been the expansion of extreme income and educational inequality in the United States and around the world, which makes it hard to envision anything like a "common" good. That's especially the case when it is combined with global patterns of immigration and movement of peoples and a host of political problems that exceed national boundaries. In these conditions, even the free speech principle, which has become a linchpin of the modern human rights program, now appears from a certain angle to be doing more to hinder the functioning of democracy or the pursuit of truth than to encourage either.

The end result, I think we need to conclude, is indeed a particular historical crisis in the relationship between democracy and truth—and one that is unlikely to end with a single dishonest American president. Surely this is not the first such crisis, and it is likely not the last. But its contours, familiar and not, call for historical as well as philosophical understanding. That's because, in threatening to erode the forms of intellectual trust and cooperation that are required for democratic life, and in making the determination of "truth" more and more obviously a consequence of brute power alone, our current practices threaten democracy itself. Even where truth is unfixed, contested, and precarious, it remains essential that it lasts as a political horizon.

Chapter 2

Experts at the Helm

"*Sapere aude!* Dare to know!": Immanuel Kant's famous dictum opens many an account of the mental revolution of the eighteenth century. Here, it seems, is *the* big idea of the age. In a few brief, essayistic pages, published in a mainstream monthly magazine no less, the great Prussian philosopher made the case for "enlightenment," not as a set of beliefs or principles but as an attitude toward truth. Maybe, most advanced philosophers agreed, one cannot know everything; the post-Lockean intellectual world is justifiably famous for its epistemological modesty, the suggestion that there are some truths—like the details of God's plan or ultimate causes—about which humans could have no certainty. But the recompense was that one *could* know an awful lot about the world and largely by finding out for oneself. True knowledge was only rarely so hard to access or esoteric in content that individuals required a particular authority—whether it be a king, a clergy member, a doctor, parents, great books, or "rules and formulas" handed down over the years until they became the prevailing wisdom—to tell them precisely what to think. What one needed, Kant declared, was primarily the "courage" to exit one's intellectual adolescence, that stage of unthinking dependency on the convictions of others, and to search for verifiable truth with an independent mind.[1]

Variants of this argument could be found all across Europe and the New World in the second half of the eighteenth century, the main starting point of the story of modern democracy and the pursuit of truth. The metaphor of illumination—of verities long covered in shadows and veils being revealed to the light of the public gaze—held, as we've seen, a special place in the progressive imaginary of the moment. So did the novel idea that this business of publicizing truth had real practical utility. From Kant to the editors of the great collaborative compendium called the *Encyclopédie,* the message was clear. The *esprit philosophique*—or what we might think of as a method of truth detection and diffusion combining reason, empiricism tied to sense experience, and a taste for questioning platitudes—would, if unhindered by censorship, lead to the perfection of most kinds of knowledge and, ultimately, the perfection of society once it had been recast in terms of this new knowledge. It was but a short step from the exposure and acknowledgment of basic truths—especially when they pertained to society—to the pursuit of ever-greater "happiness" in everyday life, as Jefferson famously framed it. The Marquis de Condorcet, writing at the height of the Terror in France in the early 1790s, remained undaunted in his conviction about the inevitability of this trajectory given humans' "zeal for the truth." The history of the future would be the story of the steady improvement of the human mind until we humans were able to talk about the moral and political sciences with all the same precision and certainty as we already talked about mathematical truths. Utopia would then lie just around the corner.[2]

It is often forgotten, however, that Kant was actually no egalitarian democrat or social leveler. Neither were most of his philosophically inclined contemporaries, including Condorcet or even Jefferson. "What Is Enlightenment?" (1784) was composed specifically for so-called men of letters. It was also focused on the job description particular to men of letters. Kant's dual subject and target audience for his exhortations to "dare to know" was ultimately a narrow slice of the population that the philosopher considered "the public." By that he meant those with the requisite knowledge base, skill as reasoners, and experience in the world necessary to help generate truth—which, de facto, also meant masculinity (with few exceptions), European urbanity, literacy in an era in which it couldn't be taken for granted, and a decent income: the kind of people who were buying and reading his essay in the *Berlinische Monatsschrift* in the first place. The *philosophes* of the Enlightenment on both sides of the Atlantic may have imagined some long-term, trickle-down effects of the spirit and method they were promoting, especially after the introduction here and there in the last decades of the eighteenth century of the idea of popular sovereignty. But they were utterly dismissive of the lower classes as currently rather hopelessly mired in stupidity, superstition, intolerance, violent emotion, and prejudice, all that enlightened sorts were, in principle, eager to transcend. As Voltaire acidly remarked in a 1764 essay on "Man": "More than half the habitable world is still populated by two-footed animals who live in a horrible condition approximating the state of nature, with hardly enough to live on and clothe themselves, barely enjoying the gift of speech, barely aware that they are miserable, living and dying practically without knowing it."[3]

Kant wasn't quite so blunt. Still, his comments to the effect that the present might be the age of the enlightenment but not yet an enlightened age suggest that he agreed with Condorcet that, much as one admired the "truly enlightened," it was important to keep in mind that they were "vastly outnumbered by the great mass of men who are still given over to ignorance and prejudice"—and thus should not be considered part of the public.[4] The charge was not that the poor and propertyless (not to mention women, the illiterate, and all others who were dependent in some way) were less likely to tell the truth or more morally inclined toward fabrication. Rather, it was that, as a result of their station in life, they lacked the ability to reason independently and thus to discern and convey the truth in the first place.[5] We might, therefore, better think of "Dare to know!" as not just the motto of an age, as Kant put it, but the mantra for a new intellectual elite situated, in the late eighteenth century, largely in Europe's capitals and port cities, including in its colonies. What defined this particular caste functionally was that it would serve the truth-related needs of society and the state, not to mention figure in the economy, in two distinct if equally valuable ways.

First, Kant, writing about men of learning, carefully made the case for the importance of doing one's appointed job, or fulfilling one's "private" function (in his parlance), well and correctly, not least when one was in the employ of an institution like the church or royal government. And by the 1780s, when Kant was writing, the number and scope of such posts, particularly in the service of the state, had already been growing at a steady clip not just in Prussia but, even more, among the great European imperial powers, France, Great Britain, and, from the start, Spain. Early modern kings, ruling often vast terrain, increasingly needed in their employ those who could manage and transmit forms of knowledge, a cohort that ranged from professors, like Kant, to librarians and archivists who controlled the growing numbers of state papers. (So much paper flowed into the court of Philip II of Spain in the sixteenth century that he became known as *el rey papelero,* or the king of paper.)[6] Kings and princes also increasingly found themselves requiring people to gather information and to create new knowledge, which is to say, uncover "useful" truths accurately and comprehensively, whether under government patronage, as in the great scientific academies created in the late seventeenth and eighteenth centuries in London, Paris, Berlin, Stockholm, and St. Petersburg, or in the direct service of rulers at court. Spies, surveyors, mapmakers, cosmographers, doctors, men adept in the new realm of political economy, explorers: these were the personnel of a burgeoning knowledge bureaucracy. Even historians, as fact-gatherers and interpreters of the past, became government fixtures in the course of the early modern era. In the 1740s, before a period in the employ of Frederick the Great in Kant's Prussia, Voltaire supported himself as "royal historiographer" at the court of Louis XV.

Eighteenth-century rulers convinced themselves that knowing more about their own people and territories, not to mention those of their enemies, past and present, would be a stimulus to internal reform projects in areas ranging from agriculture to trade to law to military aims. These same men also knew that all this new research and learning on the part of the erudite would help with conversion and the effective surveillance and management of subject populations (which largely explains why Spanish American officials also became scholars of indigenous record-keeping systems, turning them into sources for their own accounts).[7] Much as in other imperial contexts around the globe,[8] the growth and consolidation of European states, on the one hand, and the need for knowledge and, even more, knowledge-creators, on the other, went hand in hand. This is also what makes the absolutist state an important precursor to the modern, democratic one, despite our assumptions that the Age of Revolutions marked a fundamental historical break.

Kant, though, imagined a second—and newer—role for this expanding European intellectual clerisy, one that would also go on to have a long life in modern politics, especially in democracies. That was as what we now call public intellectuals (a term that did not exist in Kant's day, though he designated this function "public" in contrast with the private work of the civil servant). The job entailed mediating between the rest of the population and the powers that be, but also acting as a kind of intellectual and ethical watchdog. In this second capacity, his *Gelehrters* or scholars would, individually and collectively, be less deferential to political or clerical authority. Rather, inside the special, extrapolitical space of the so-called republic of letters and freed from ordinary restrictions on the circulation of ideas, they would be emboldened to speak truth to power, to use a modern colloquialism—though Kant warned that this could not happen in the workplace, only in the afterhours, when one was free to "make a *public use* of one's reason in all matters" and to write in the increasingly market-based press that ruled this imaginary republic.[9]

His example of a military officer makes the distinction clear. An officer must refrain while on the job from quibbling about the appropriateness or utility of any order he receives; he must simply obey. Still, Kant continued, "he cannot fairly be forbidden as a scholar to make remarks on failings in the military service and to lay them before the public for judgment."[10] As such, the officer, acting in his public capacity, could be seen as the precursor to the independent journalist of today, only operating in an era before anyone imagined any real distinction between the investigative reporter uncovering the facts and the engaged political commentator. His social responsibility was skepticism about all official versions of truth; he had to dare to know. The ultimate goal, though, was not to undermine faith in the existence of truth per se. Rather, it was to help in the collective process of bringing the demonstrable truth ever more visibly into the light in an era when state secrecy and censorship were still the norm. That, and to spread the habit of weighing all ideas critically even more broadly into the "reading world" or burgeoning realm of enlightened public opinion.

Whether one person could or can really fulfill both functions at once—creating and maintaining useful truths as a state agent subject to bosses *and* questioning official truth as an independent member of the republic of letters before the tribunal of public opinion—is an interesting question. It's also one that, as we will see, does not go away, especially in the age of social media. Voltaire found it highly fraught and well-nigh impossible during his stint as court historian in chief. Any number of Twitter-based controversies involving salaried professors' contentious off-hours, online comments suggest that it still is.

What matters first for our purposes, however, is simply the long shadow cast over the modern world by the emergence of this enlightened case for the social and political utility of a distinct cohort of the learned. For here, in the Kantian Enlightenment ideal, we can see the makings of new class lines established around the determination and expression of truth. Certainly the idea grew in stature in eighteenth-century Europe and the New World, and especially in areas marked by Protestantism or heterodoxy, that, in principle, all people naturally possess a common capacity to grasp, on their own, the basic features of the world around them. (It is difficult to imagine anyone taking seriously the possibility of republican governance without holding this prior conviction about human nature.) This notion has remained vital to social justice movements ever since, as well as the current of populist politics that will be the subject of the next chapter. But the earliest of the modern experiments in instituting popular self-rule were constructed largely by enlightened types in ways designed precisely to *prevent* ordinary men, not to mention women of all classes, the poor, the nonwhite, the enslaved, the foreign, and the truly indigenous, from having too much power to impose their vision of the external world either as it had existed or as it should. What comes to be the modern form of democracy has inscribed within it an abstract commitment to equality and commonality around rights and even basic conceptions of human nature, right along with new forms of "natural" social distinction.

That included an idea of a moral (which would soon drop out) and intellectual (which would last) meritocracy—to use an anachronistic term—that has never been separable from money and property, education, and social standing, which has thus traditionally involved assumptions about gender, race, ethnicity, and religious identity too.

Even in republics, where the people as a whole were deemed sovereign and where hierarchies built around both kings and formal aristocracies with hereditary titles were declared unlawful, it was widely acknowledged in the late eighteenth century that statecraft required a distinct political class characterized by exceptional wisdom and virtue. Practically speaking, that meant men with some formal knowledge, whether by schooling or proper experience, of the principles of governing and a commitment to giving and keeping their word as an element of gentlemanly honor.[11] Or at least it did by the architects of early republics in British North America and then France, who themselves tended to belong to that very class.

The so-called Federalists, or advocates of the federal Constitution in the new United States, were particularly committed to this notion, sparring repeatedly on these grounds with the less hierarchical anti-Federalists and then Democratic-Republicans in the republic's early years. Consider the Enlightenment-inspired logic of Alexander Addison, a Federalist judge from Pennsylvania. For him it was axiomatic circa 1800 that ordinary people were, under present conditions, deficient as judges of public matters, "too apt to confound right with capacity, and power with skill." But those who understood that "the art of governing, is a science," meaning a discipline rooted in the pursuit of sure truths and effective, demonstrable methods for verifying them, and had the requisite "knowledge, study, and reflection" (which surely also indicated social standing and leisure time) to approach politics in this manner, could compensate for others' cognitive, not to mention ethical, limitations.[12] It was, therefore, important that power in practice be accorded disproportionately to a particular and new kind of elite of the talented, even as "the people" were, abstractly, possessed of sovereignty and the power to judge. In effect, this view amounted to not much more than a rehash of Madison's famous words in Federalist 57: "The aim of every political constitution is or ought to be first to obtain for rulers men who possess [the] most wisdom to discern, and [the] most virtue to pursue, the common good of the society," since one could hardly expect to luck upon (as noted in Federalist 49) "a nation of philosophers." Or, as a more straightforward Roger Sherman of Connecticut put it while debating the Constitution in Philadelphia in 1787, "the people . . . should have as little to do as may be about the Government."[13]

Ultimately, this logic manifested itself in almost every aspect of the official culture of the early U.S. republic, initiating tensions that last to this day in the working out of the relationship of democracy to truth. Take voting. In principle, elections were to be a central and regular feature of American governance; they allowed both states and the nation not only to make concrete the notion of the sovereignty of the people, but also to gauge their collective judgments about what had happened in the past and what their preferences were for the future. And by establishing a process based on the idea of one person, one vote, every enfranchised citizen was theoretically to be accorded an equally valuable voice in all such determinations. But the voting public was always imagined as a restricted body. In practice, fear of "mob rule," which especially after the start of the French Revolution conjured up anarchy as well as a general assault on the rights of property owners, ensured the continuation of stringent suffrage and office-holding requirements left over from the Colonial Era. The disenfranchisement of the propertyless, as well as all youths, all women, and all native and black men in most places in the new United States, marked the endurance of the old idea that financial independence (originally, holding sufficient income-producing land as head of a household) was a prerequisite for intellectual independence, meaning an ability to think for oneself or, in Kant's parlance, "to dare to know." What those who lacked independence in this double sense owed those who had it was deference in the realm of ideas, including political ones.[14]

Furthermore, even as property requirements started to fall state-by-state between the 1790s and the 1850s and voting became perceived more as a right than privilege, racial barriers and gender barriers, sometimes framed around literacy standards or quasi-scientific arguments about inferior intellectual competency, became more entrenched. The Constitution itself initially authorized direct voting at the federal level only for members of the House of Representatives. Complex forms of suffrage involving various kinds and layers of electors would, it was thought, further insulate the republic from "the violence of the majority faction," or dependency on the unchecked aspirations and worldviews of ordinary people, and help to ensure that the more predictable and universal wisdom and values of the richer, the better educated, and the more socially distinguished would dominate.[15] The Electoral

College, a vestige of this way of thinking, remains operative for presidential elections today.

Or consider education in the early U.S. republic. In principle, as almost every Founding Father explained, education and citizenship went together—and in a way that was quite different from the relationship they had had in monarchies or even in the colonial period in North America. Expanded educational opportunities were thought necessary if ordinary people were to participate in democracy in a full way, evaluating ideas and people, debating them, and then choosing. But just as much, schools and schooling seemed essential to preventing those same people from being deceived or led down false paths by the deliberately deceptive and dangerous, that is, those who might prey on the people's credulity. Instruction—especially in the basic principles of right and wrong, true and false—could, following old Radical Whig logic, be considered a form of inoculation, a way to ensure that "the people" would, in fact, see through the lies of would-be flatterers, panderers, and those, in Alexander Hamilton's words in Federalist 68, with "talents for low intrigue." By these measures, even women would need formal training since they would be responsible for molding the next generation of active republicans.

Yet, again in practice, ordinary people in the new United States had little access to anything beyond very basic education well into the nineteenth century, and those outside the political community, including almost all Native Americans and African Americans, had none. Taxpayers were largely unwilling to support the education of others who were not their own children, seeing little civic benefit, especially if those people weren't going to

have to judge public questions on their own. Life experience was widely deemed a sufficient, even preferable, form
of education for most ordinary citizens. Indeed, many
elites also actively worried about instructing people in
ideas that were conceptually beyond their current station,
seeing in the practice not the possibility of social mobility
but rather of social unrest. This was an old idea too: Cardi-
nal Richelieu, in his *Testament politique* offering his advice
to France's Louis XIII, had insisted back in the seventeenth
century that knowledge raises expectations in dangerous
ways that inevitably leave people discontented with their
lot, and the encyclopedist René D'Alembert a century later
had explained that, in fact, the multitude would likely find
sudden exposure to "the truth" (*la vérité*) a provocation.[16]

So, instead, American intellectual elites in the early
republic tended to promote hierarchical visions of education, including special plans for molding the exclusive
governing class of representatives and their intellectual
support networks that the new republic required. The Federalist Benjamin Rush, already alarmed in 1776 by all the
"unknown" men scrambling for political positions in his
home state of Pennsylvania, went on record proposing the
creation of a national university designed specifically to
train a corps of certified civil servants, men with special
"obligations to wisdom and integrity," in applied science,
commerce and manufacturing, history, "federal principles," and other subjects important to statecraft, yet again
a vision with roots in early modern European states.[17]
If we don't let pilots guide ships without certification,
he asked rhetorically, "why then should we commit our
country . . . to men who cannot produce vouchers of their
qualifications for this important trust?" This dedication

to the formation of a special, credentialed political class cannot, though, simply be attributed to the social conservatism of the Federalists. For Rush's chief complaint was actually the potentially reactionary nature of the crowd, which he perceived as weighed down by its longstanding prejudices, unable to appreciate innovation, and fated to endlessly prop up the status quo if not succumb to despotism. To his mind, only men of real knowledge could break through the cycle of habit and custom to create rational policy together.

And though Rush's national educational plan was rejected as simply *too* elitist by the Founding generation, even his staunch political opponent, Thomas Jefferson, wasn't so sure that Rush had it all wrong. Believing it essential for states to cultivate what he called a "natural aristocracy" specifically for the "trusts of government," Jefferson continually made the case from the late 1770s onward for a multitiered educational system in the states. General and widespread education would help prevent the rise of despots and demagogues, and history instruction in particular promised to inculcate in the young the ability to act "as judges of the actions and designs of men," a key civic function.[18] But Jefferson (and Madison too) hoped the people would then elect to be ruled by the "best" among them. Thus Jefferson insisted on the importance of mechanisms for seeking out those of talent or merit across all social ranks and cultivating them in special institutions dedicated to forming enlightened political leadership (which led the more cynical John Adams to claim that this educational elite would always end up coinciding with oligarchy since, in a commercial republic, the people themselves would likely continue to remain dazzled by wealth and family name, not just some abstract notion of merit).[19] Both proved right, as secondary schools and colleges, though never a national university, proliferated to take on this job, conferring new status on old elites along with a smattering of newcomers—just as they arguably still do.[20] The "university man" would, by the mid-nineteenth century, become a pejorative, a synonym in American political rhetoric for the eggheaded snob, *and* a model for the wise, the knowledgeable, the well-situated, and the trustworthy.[21]

Even early debates and policies on the role of the press in a republic followed this pattern. As we've seen in chapter one, the First Amendment to the Constitution built on colonial and English precedents to remove the state from the business of determining, through either repressive censorship or propaganda production, what is false and what is true. The law was intended to stimulate the pursuit of truth by allowing ideas of all kinds to fight it out for the public's attention in a growing commercial marketplace and, ultimately, for the imprimatur of being termed accepted, verifiable knowledge by a heterodox public. Here too, though, almost immediately the open-endedness of the First Amendment in all its brevity, along with the emergence of a highly vituperative public sphere riven with partisan animosity, produced new anxieties similar to those of today. That was especially the case among Federalists, who declared themselves shocked, *shocked* by all the mudslinging and rival truth-claims. If, they reasoned, the people were still malleable and open to demagoguery, falsehood, and manipulation, and if the press itself were dishonest and replete with invective and disinformation, how could one be convinced that, without some regulation or formal engineering, the real truth would, in fact, ultimately prevail? As the Federalist-allied *Albany Centinel* colorfully put it in 1798, Republicans would keep propagating "lies and liars, as a hot day breeds maggots or musketoes," and the people would surely be led astray, unsure whom to believe in the end.[22]

Amidst a larger power struggle, the Alien and Sedition Acts of 1798 can be read as the Federalists' early push to restore some of the prerogative of the state and its spokesmen in establishing what counts as truth. In practice, that meant bolstering those (surely equally partisan) notions that they saw as meeting the standard of veracity and eliminating from view what did not. The Acts were also short lived, at least in terms of the part that concerned sedition, a casualty of the Federalists' defeat in 1800. It is important to keep in mind, though, that the much more expansive view of the First Amendment held today, which has lately been used to support practices ranging from the propagation of scientifically unverified claims by "pregnancy centers" to the deregulation of campaign financing, is almost entirely a creation of twentieth- and twenty-first-century jurisprudence. Many once thought, like our Judge Addison, "Truth has but one side, and listening to error and falsehood is indeed a strange way to discover truth."[23] Even Jefferson, who largely kept faith in the (relative) superiority of public determinations about truth and falsehood over those of judges and political leaders, wondered privately if mankind might actually be better off without newspapers since "as vehicles of information, and a curb on our functionaries, they have rendered themselves useless, by forfeiting all title to belief."[24] In addition, arguably up to the age of the Internet, markets have effectively served as a different kind of public censor, subtly controlling with dollars what gets said and, even more, what gets heard in the public sphere. Republics have never really meant that all views will, in the political realm, garner equal weight or attention.

Indeed, in the aftermath of the Terror of the French Revolution, the leaders of France's governments of the mid- to late 1790s tried to do many of the same things as the Federalists to keep republicanism—as opposed to pure democracy—alive. The initial step entailed beating back what were perceived as the dual threats of royalist fanaticism on the right and of Jacobin democratic extremism on the left. The second was to turn Robespierre's "republic of virtue" into a republic of reason, or shift the form and locus of truth within the framework of popular sovereignty. The project transpired on multiple fronts.

Repudiating a brief experiment with universal manhood suffrage in 1793, the French authors of the Constitution of Year III (1795) once again restricted the franchise, as well as upped the requirements for office holding, this time in an effort to limit the say of potential radicals. Distinctions between "active" and "passive" citizens rooted in financial "independence," or property qualifications, returned, and the law (though it was never put into effect) soon attached the rights of citizenship to knowledge of written French, an educational threshold, as well. The leadership of the Thermidorean Republic and the Directory also began subsidizing worthy publications and building new, elite training grounds. That included a so-called Normal School (*École normale*), the first dedicated to teaching teachers sure methods for getting students to arrive at truths—or what Americans would later in the nineteenth century call the "science of learning."[25]

Napoleon, even as he reversed many of the liberal trends of the early 1790s, including restoring an extensive censorship apparatus aimed at newspapers and other forms of public expression in an effort to further control public conversation, would go on to expand the higher education system in France and to create (and export) the *lycée* or high school system that lasts to this day.[26]

One real hope behind all this educational institution building in France in the mid- and late-1790s was that it would generate a new language for politics, an idiom that catered less to the passions than to reason and thereby gave the political leaders of the moment greater control over the realm of truth. Well before the Terror, Enlightenment *philosophes* like Condorcet and the Abbé de Condillac had promised that "all sciences would be exact if we only knew how to speak the language of each." Afterward, leading Idéologue philosophers and political figures attached to the new Normal School, like Dominique-Joseph Garat, declared that the time had now finally arrived to realize this dream—and in the political sphere as well as in a purely scientific one. For with the aid of the proper language, as would be developed and taught at this innovative school, the "moral sciences, so necessary to people who govern themselves by their own virtues," would finally be "subjected to proofs as rigorous as those in the exact and physical sciences." Then, he promised, both certainty about basic principles (rather than debate) and social harmony (rather than strife) would result. The proceedings of the school and other important new institutions of the era would even be recorded by a new technical aid called stenography—an eighteenth-century practice that the Trump White House has just brought to a halt—so that reading the transcripts, "one can say with assurance: here is the truth."[27]

But all these new schools and this intense focus on advanced pedagogy had a second function: creating a new, post-Jacobin, French intellectual elite who would become adept at these methods and shape the content and meaning of this new language of political truths. If earlier revolutionaries had been committed to obscurantism and the obfuscation of the truth (as the Thermidoreans and Directorials insisted after the fact), they would be replaced by *philosophe*-legislators, devotees of rational administration tainted neither by aristocracy nor by popular democracy in their views of the world. Should we be surprised that the Thermidorean Convention, which dates from right after Robespierre's demise, took as its guidepost Condorcet's great *Esquisse* and voted to publish and distribute to the public three thousand copies of this text in which the last great *philosophe* foresaw a day in which the only social distinction remaining would be between "men of learning and upright men who know the value of learning without being dazzled by it; or between talent or genius and the common sense which can appreciate and benefit from them ... [in] promoting what is advantageous for their independence and happiness"?[28] Soon thereafter Madame de Staël would propose, in the same spirit as Jefferson's "natural aristocracy," that a stable republic required nothing less than *une aristocratie des meilleurs,* meaning one chamber in a bicameral system of government that explicitly placed power in the hands of "the most enlightened, most virtuous, and most courageous" members of society.[29] Standing above factional conflict, this elite (and unelected) body would be able to focus exclusively on the general good and root out all that was dangerous or false—just as a republic required.

In the end, the French version of this story, it is important to note, is considerably more statist than the American one. In the United States, the liberation of most constraints on public expression, combined with the growth of a host of private efforts and voluntary movements aimed at self-improvement, seemed more attractive for most of the nineteenth century than the building of new state institutions, especially when it came to questions of knowledge production or dissemination. By contrast, the government of France, and, eventually, those of Great Britain, Germany, and Russia too put considerably more energy and state money into the sponsorship of research and the development of new areas of knowledge in the nineteenth century.[30] France also maintained greater state control over the circulation of ideas and betrayed more enthusiasm, at least in the immediate aftermath of the Revolution, for the idea that it would one day be possible to make politics an exact science. It is, though, the shared goals of early republican leaders, European and American alike, that draw our attention: combining the idea of the rule of the people with a truth-regime in which a particular, well-trained elite sector is primarily entrusted with defining both the how and the what.

Of course, that said, democracy did take off in the new century. The story of the nineteenth century on both sides of the Atlantic is eventually the story of the rise of mass politics spurred by the joint explosion of industrial capitalism and democracy (which, in the course of the first decades of the new century, lost its pejorative associations for its many advocates). From Jacksonians in the United States, to Chartists in England, to radicals and socialists across much of the European continent and Latin America, "democrats"—sometimes in conjunction with and sometimes in opposition to reform-minded liberals who sought constitutional monarchies or other, more top-down forms of rule—clamored for and eventually got in the course of the next century and a half most of the things that the Founding Fathers were so eager to withhold.

The nineteenth century saw the eventual end of chattel slavery in the West and the steady (if hotly contested) expansion of voting rights, culminating in universal manhood suffrage in much of North and South America, Australia and New Zealand, and much of Western Europe, including Britain, France, Belgium, and the new states of Italy and Germany, albeit often with limits on voting by racial or ethnic minorities and a standard failure to enact universal female suffrage that lasted in most places well past World War I. That same century also saw the growth of state-funded schooling, as well as the expansion of other kinds of popular educational institutions, from museums to public libraries. In many states, primary education became compulsory for young citizens in the making too (though for reasons usually having more to do with social control and national identity formation than human rights). With the rise of formal political parties of distinct ideological stripes, mass involvement in politics became the norm as well. So did the explosion of the press in capitalist marketplaces in which more and more different versions of the news found themselves in competition, increasingly unimpeded by much government regulation, and with churches or any other institutions less and less able to impose any single doc-trine or dogma on an expanding public. By 1849, in Paris alone, one could find 450 different papers for sale, all with their own takes on the news of the day.[31] Something simi-lar happened in the revolutionary states of Rome, Venice, and Vienna, as well as in Mexico City and Buenos Aires after independence. By the end of the century, circulation had turned mass too, a product of rising literacy but also of the falling price of print.

All of these institutions served new epistemic func-tions, namely, involving ordinary people in making truth determinations in the public sphere. At the same time, leaders of liberalizing or democratic movements, includ-ing politicians, congratulated themselves on their moral rectitude and their taste for transparency in their dealings with the public and with one another. In some cases, as in England, that also meant steadily expanding laws to pre-vent corruption, or cover-ups of self-dealing, along with the definition of corruption itself; on both sides of the Atlantic, honesty became prized as much as a middle-class virtue as a gentlemanly one.[32] Even when talking about states that remained on the eve of World War I liberal constitutional monarchies as opposed to democracies or republics, we can speak freely about the democratization of truth and truth-related values after their rather socially circumscribed beginnings.

However, in a first major irony, it turned out that lib-eral and newly democratic states, under the conditions of capitalism, required even more by way of "useful knowl-edge" than more traditional ones ever did. That was in good part to help solve the new and manifold problems that industrial capitalism, when abetted by liberal democracy, created in its wake. Information-driven improvement schemes typical of enlightened monarchs and early republics morphed in the course of the nineteenth century into formal "policy-making" on topics ranging from trade to crime to labor conditions, that is, new areas of human welfare. As a result, the practice of political decision-making became ever more dependent upon basic truths spelled out by elites in their capacity as "experts" (as they were first termed in Anglophone and French settings in the nineteenth century) and *Fachmann* (as German speakers called them at the same moment). These were people whose long and specific "experience" made them exceptionally credible when it came to telling others what had transpired—or what Arendt would call empirical truths— and what was likely to work in the future.[33] Governments in countries with rapidly expanding populations and economic sectors soon couldn't do without them.

That was the case even in the United States, where the myth of the small, restrained state lasting from the Founding until the rupture of the New Deal in the 1930s remains prevalent despite much historical evidence to the contrary. Fundamental to American politics has long been not just the assumption that the president and members of Congress, as well as civil servants, will be honest about their own dealings—indeed, that honesty, as for George Washington of the "I cannot tell a lie" cherry tree legend, will be a primary virtue of the political ruling class.[34] We have also been led to believe (at least until recently) that elected and appointed officials at every level will encourage, relay, and build on truthful information, based on the latest, publicly available learning. (Benjamin Franklin, the diplomat and inventor, was, of course, another hero of the age.) Furthermore, they will do so at every turn, whether the topic is native languages or farming techniques or financial regulation.[35]

Consider the census as a form of federally sponsored knowledge production in which the new American republic actually once led the way.[36] Article 1, Section 2 of the U.S. Constitution established the requirement, starting in 1790, of a decennial fact-finding mission focused on population changes across the states (a counterpart perhaps to Lewis and Clark's slightly later information-gathering exploration of the natural world, which was understood to include native peoples). Other censuses had been done before, including, in previous decades, in Sweden, Denmark, Norway, and Spain, which had also long collected data about natural and human life in the New World. The idea for a descriptive accounting of the population by way of survey goes back to ancient Rome and continued with the Catholic Church's censuses of souls. But the U.S. Constitution turned the census, for the first time, into a permanent government institution and a source of public knowledge, a practice that would quickly spread to France, Great Britain, and well beyond in the first half of the nineteenth century. The idea was that government could not fulfill its basic functions without a series of time-specific snapshots that revealed the inevitable shifts in the makeup and the geographic distribution of the nation's population. The enterprise also draws our attention now, though, because it exhibits several of the key characteristics of the distinctive relationship between knowledge claims, on the one hand, and the development of democracy, on the other, that were to become characteristic of the nineteenth century across much of the West.

First, the United States census belongs from the start to the blossoming postrevolutionary trend of thinking of real knowledge as scientific in nature and, even more, "statistical," another word that only grew in popularity as it expanded beyond its original meaning (literally, information of use to states). Indeed, the federal census, whose scope and mathematical foundations developed in tandem, is here only representative of this larger trend. The word "statisticks" first cropped up in an American dictionary in 1803.[37] It then took off fast. As early as 1818, a Pennsylvania representative named Adam Seybert managed to publish an eight-hundred–page tome that shared almost all the statistical data that had been collected to date by the federal government, not to mention some state and local ones. The title of this history in numbers? *Statistical Annals: Embracing Views of the Population, Commerce, Navigation, Fisheries, Public Lands, Post-Office Establishment, Revenues, Mint, Military and Naval Establishments, Expenditures, Public Debt and Sinking Fund, of the United States of America, Founded on Official Documents, 1789–1818.*[38] Popular gazettes and almanacs similarly presented interested citizens with portraits of the world in hard numbers. Soon, statistical societies and bureaus were taking root in Europe and the United States alike, collecting, classifying, and analyzing data on questions from rates of insanity to the state of child welfare, areas far beyond the population and industry metrics typically captured by the first modern censuses. Historian Gordon Wood says we might even speak of "fact-collecting" as a new national obsession in the early republic, though the United States was hardly alone.[39] By the late nineteenth century, the study of such data had become a German academic field unto itself and a foundation for all the other so-called "social sciences," including politics, much as Condorcet had once hoped.

What was the appeal of the language of statistics, or "political arithmetic," as it was also known? We should see this craze for quantification as part of the spurning of subjectivity or personal judgment that was characteristic of nineteenth-century science more broadly. Statistics, such as those derived from census data, seemed to show things *as they really are,* without the interests or biases or even judgments of (increasingly unknown) information-providers creeping in and distorting things.[40] If democracy, by definition, included a "moral demand for impartiality and fairness," it was answered more and more in the nineteenth century, according to historian Theodore Porter, with the idea of "objectivity": the neutral methods and values of natural science transferred to the study of social and moral phenomena in pursuit of an exact representation of the external world. Here was, ostensibly, the "plain," transparent, bias-free, simplified form of speech that language reformers in France and elsewhere had long sought. Statistics promised to be an aid in law- and policy-making, yes, but also a way of presenting and justifying decisions, a "technology of trust" in instances when one had no personal knowledge of the people offering up what were promised as incontrovertible truths.[41] They made every aspect of life a matter of precise calculation. (That is certainly why statistics appealed to advocates of industrial capitalism as well, as Marx and Engels already noted in 1848.)[42]

That said, the second trend associated with the census returns our focus to people, particularly the people behind all those numbers. As the nature of what was being measured got increasingly complicated and there seemed always to be more information to gather, discern, and record, essential work—on the census and on similar nineteenth-century data-driven projects—was done more and more by "professionals" and "specialists," new terms for those with an assumed special relationship to objective truth by virtue of their exclusive training and specialized areas of competency.[43] In the course of the nineteenth century, the division of labor that characterized other fields came to knowledge production too. Generalists and amateurs—the "wise" men of the Founding Era and its learned societies—gave way to experts in specific domains, each with their own courses of study, associations, journals, congresses, even ways of expressing themselves, all of which also marked their difference from laypeople, from clergymen (even if these new experts were sometimes thought to constitute a "scientific priesthood" and their ranks once overlapped), and even from legislators and elected representatives. The U.S. census followed this path. In 1850, for example, just as the nation was threatening to unravel in strife connected to slavery, the census finally became ensconced in a formal statistical office within the Department of the Interior, and a battalion of salaried, professional clerks were hired with the task of tabulating and publishing the results.[44] But this was no longer the vanguard. Starting in the prior decade, it was really German science, or *Wissenschaft*, that led the way in creating new, international contours for knowledge production, including in the creation of new kinds of knowledge professionals—a development that would reshape democratic politics all the way to the American West despite its undemocratic place of origins.

On the one hand, all this professional specialization in the realm of knowledge had the potential to drive a further social wedge between classes, especially as it got harder and harder to evaluate or even comprehend anyone else's conclusions, or how they came to them, from the outside. Doctors, engineers, various other kinds of "scientists" (yet another nineteenth-century neologism on the knowledge front): the tendency was increasingly to generate research findings by means and in forms, including statistical ones, that were largely incomprehensible to ordinary people, but also often incomprehensible across different professional fields. Many educated people, it seemed, knew more than ever about less and less. On the other hand, one could increasingly look to title, institutional affiliation, and credentials and make some assumptions—or so it was hoped by training and licensing bodies—about the extent of those individuals' knowledge of the matter at hand and also their ethical code. That code typically entailed a commitment to rigor in method (over guesswork or instinct), to impartiality (over prejudice or political or religious biases), to the dry, technical presentation of facts (over emotionalism or sensationalism), and to public service (over pocketbook or marketplace concerns). These became the presumed defining features of nineteenth-century knowledge professionalism across multiple fields.

It was this combination, as opposed to indices of personal virtue, that ostensibly gave these often faceless experts a particular right to be believed as truth-purveyors.[45] The legitimacy of government reform projects—whether social, economic, or military—stemmed in part from the epistemic authority of new knowledge specialists, from statisticians to engineers, and their ostensible commitment to unvarnished, if often fairly incomprehensible, truth. (It still helps today when something can be seen to be backed by good scientific research—hence, for example, the desire for gun-control advocates to get the National Institutes of Health back in the game of studying gun violence—though that impulse may be fading.) But scientific experts also gained status of their own by associating themselves with prestigious state projects and patronage. With their portable credentials, some of these professionals also thrived in the highly competitive world of industrial capitalism.

This happened, moreover, on both national and international scales. Expertise-driven projects extended in the nineteenth century to colonial contexts, whether via experts exported for the purpose to Algiers or Delhi, or via reliance on local, non-European elites. Imperialism and the invention of environmental, medical, racial, linguistic, and anthropological expertise went hand in hand.[46] The appeal of European-style expertise also traveled, often attached to positivist notions advanced by Henri de Saint-Simon and then Auguste Comte, well outside of Europe's immediate orbit. Think of Porfirio Diáz and his *científicos,* or technical advisors, trying to "modernize" Mexico in the 1870s and 1880s.[47] Or consider the growing influence of scientific experts in Japanese government offices, stoked by French positivist notions of the coming triumph of the verifiable fact.[48] Everywhere by the late nineteenth century the forces of professionalism and specialization, aided by industry and the state, seemingly pulled experts, as something more and more like a class, even further from ordinary people in the realm of knowledge.

Furthermore, there was actually no escaping the political in any of this, no matter what these experts seemed to be objectively counting or recording or informing others about. On the contrary, to return to the example of the American census, the issues could not have been more heated from the start. How could it have been otherwise when what was at stake, on a national scale, was the distribution of political power, the allocation of revenue, and behind it all up through the Civil War, the continued existence of chattel slavery and the status of the enslaved as people to be counted or something else? Every question, every category or classification that made its way into the census had political implications. The design of the whole, starting with names and definitions, was necessarily just as political as the implementation or the analysis that followed. Even the choice of mathematical methods proved contentious in the nineteenth century, as some techniques ultimately favored bigger states and some favored smaller ones.

Bickering over the census' constituent elements and execution also continues to this day, just like arguments about the science behind gun violence, based both on the assumption that the self-interest of politicians cannot be so easily separated from the objective knowledge of the experts and on the idea that there are some things that parts of the public has reason not to want to know. The French, for example, do not ask about race on their national census so as to avoid exacerbating divisions within the population, while Americans see racial categories as important in providing minority groups with social recognition, even though the names and number of those categories are always up for debate. At the moment of this book's composition, a seemingly innocuous, fact-finding question about citizenship status added to the 2020 census by the Trump administration has become a new battleground. Some people, including most social scientists and advocates for immigrants, insist that asking it will ultimately compromise the veracity of the whole by reducing participation rates among the undocumented, which in turn will have serious implications in terms of undercounting and thus underfunding and underrepresenting certain cities and states. Others say that the new question should be seen as no more than a way to garner useful, impartial information.[49] Neutrality is, though, rarely attainable in such situations. That's true even when it comes to facts that can be investigated empirically. For whether we are talking about foreign policy or the economy or any other area of government interest, statistical categories reflect previous political choices (think again of the so-called unemployment rate). They also produce political effects, sometimes creating reality as much as describing it. Facts and interpretations, which means politics, are inevitably tied up in one another from the start.

Is this, then, a fatal flaw of expert knowledge and, by extension, the modern way to truth? Must even the most rigorously determined objective facts, established by professionals, turn into political footballs in democratic settings? At the close of the nineteenth century and several decades into the new one, an international group of reformers known as Progressives imagined that the excessive politicization of knowledge, not to mention the rot of public corruption, could indeed be overcome with the right methods and forms of collaboration. To do so properly would mean finally to realize the cooperative epistemic dream at the heart of the democratic idea.

John Dewey, perhaps the greatest American philosopher of the era, made the case with relish. Progressives like Dewey were convinced, following an earlier generation of Pragmatists, that no fixed or timeless truths existed. On the contrary: knowledge is necessarily social in its construction, as in its verification, and all findings must be treated as revisable based on experiment or experience. In this spirit, Progressives also tended to advocate the amping up of democratization, calling for more civic education, more public debate, and more direct measures for the expression of popular sentiments, including primaries, ballot initiatives, and referenda. That, and the dismantling of corruption from on high. At the same time, though, Dewey and company uniformly placed great faith, for the future of politics, in the model of the sciences. Indeed, he saw remarkable synergy between democratic decision-making and the procedures of the natural sciences, especially when it came to the establishment of truths.

In 1899, Dewey claimed democracy "implies tools for getting at truth in detail, and day by day, as we go along," and thus it also required "alignment with science."[50] In 1927, he was still insisting that political life was suffering from "an absence of facts," and there was a need "to raise the level upon which the intelligence of all operates."[51] That meant that Dewey and his allies also placed a considerable amount of trust in public-minded scientific elites, those authorities in truly experiential, collaborative, yet disinterested methods of truth construction, in working against "secrecy" and "bias" and "misrepresentation" and "propaganda" and in providing the knowledge and know-how necessary for effective government. In the ideal world, those public-minded experts would not frame or decide on policies; that would be a problem for laypeople. But experts would discover and make known all the facts upon which good policy depends, and crucially, they would also establish the grounds for public debate. Moreover, science would provide the ethical values that democracy requires without impinging on popular participation. As Dewey himself explained it in *The Public and Its Problems* (1927),

> No government by experts in which the masses do not have the chance to inform the experts as to their needs can be anything but an oligarchy managed in the interests of the few. . . . [But] the essential need . . . is the improvement of the methods and conditions of debate, discussion, and persuasion. That is *the* problem of the public. We have asserted that this improvement depends essentially upon freeing and perfecting the processes of inquiry and of dissemination of their conclusions. Inquiry, indeed, is a link that devolves upon experts. But their expertness is not in framing and executing policies, but in discovering and making known the facts upon which the former depend. They are technical experts in the sense that scientific investigators and artists manifest *expertise*.[52]

We should hear strong echoes here of the Enlightenment, albeit in the new language of Dewey's moment. At the end of the day Dewey seems more to have been renewing and updating a tradition of enlightened epistemology visible at the origins of the first republics than breaking the mold. His vision also proved powerful, especially in the aftermath of World War I. From the 1890s through the 1920s, Europeans and Americans bore witness to the inauguration of the much expanded modern, administrative state. And while some new kinds of professional administrators and civil servants were hired to bring more integrity and oversight into public life, others were tasked with pressing into service new kinds of social scientific data gathered by teams of experts in German-inspired "research universities," as well as within the ranks of the state administrative apparatus, that could help in addressing the welfare of citizens. Think how much the provision of insurance and old-age pensions or the introduction of protections for workers on both American and British shores depended upon new forms and institutional sources of "objective," vetted information.[53] In the words of the British Liberal imperialist Viscount Haldane just after the turn of the new century, "What is true of commerce and industry is not less true of the Art of Government. This art is founded on science. When the clear conceptions which science alone can give are absent, confusion is the result. Our best reformers in such subjects as Poor Law administration, in Education, in Local Government, in . . . Trade, in Public Health, and last, but not least, in Railway administration, are yearly insisting more loudly on the necessity for the trained mind."[54]

Meanwhile, on the other side of the Atlantic, turn-of-the-century Americans pointed to states like Wisconsin as nothing less than "laboratories" for democracy as a result of progressive partnerships for policy-making among professors and scientists working at state universities, legislators, and the public.[55] This was also the era of the rise of independent news and investigative, "muckraking" (as Theodore Roosevelt termed them) photographers and journalists, determined to expose the truth of the present in factual ways, apart from party politics.[56] Ida B. Wells, whose successful career as a journalist and antilynching activist in the 1890s was even more remarkable given that she had neither race nor gender on her side in her bid for expertise, gave expression to this ethos when she insisted in the conclusion to *The Red Record,* "The answer [for to how to make a difference] is always 'tell the world the facts.'"[57] Frederick Douglass echoed this conviction in the letter that fronted Wells's extraordinary book: "I have spoken, but my word is feeble in comparison. You give us what you know and testify from actual knowledge. You have dealt with the facts with cool, painstaking fidelity, and left those naked and uncontradicted facts to speak for themselves." But the ultimate symbol of this age of faith in facticity might be polygraph experts, white men who promised to bring similar scientific rigor to ferreting out truth and untruth in the courtroom by turning to a decidedly dispassionate tool: the newly invented machine known as a lie-detector.[58]

Nevertheless, striking this imagined balance between experts and laypeople had its challenges, especially as the era of the polygraph was also that of the sensationalizing "yellow" press and rising nationalism and xenophobia. Running through Progressive thought and policy were always hints that advantage *might* be found in sometimes letting experts supersede public judgments, especially when the former "knew better" than the latter. Consider that, in a bid to rid cities of the corruption associated with party machines, elected mayors of small cities in the United States began in the 1910s, with Progressive backing, to give way to unelected "city managers."[59] Appointing men characterized distinctively by "honesty, system, fairness, harmony [and] expertness" (in the words of the city manager of Abilene, Texas, who was quoted in a 1914 article on this "new profession") promised to bring nothing less than the modern values of "efficiency and economy" to municipal government.[60] What did not get said is that such positions also offered no way for the public to hold such ostensibly apolitical policymakers accountable.

Moreover, in theory too, late nineteenth– and early twentieth–century Progressives, every bit as much as authoritarians, could find themselves moving away from an attachment to democracy in a literal sense. Though social democrats like the turn-of-the century English Fabians Beatrice and Sidney Webb always insisted on their commitment to popular rule, they too ended up tempted in both theory and practice by the idea of carving out space for new forms of expert judgment, including specialists and trained administrators, and social control. Much like Benjamin Rush a hundred years earlier, in other words, this enlightened couple did not really believe that the people, compromised by ignorance and a kind of false consciousness that came with having accepted the status quo in an era of organized capitalist oligarchy, could really be counted on to recognize or act on their own best interest. Or at least not without guidance from above in the form of people like themselves! The old method of getting to the common good by letting the whole population fight it out simply didn't work anymore, it seemed.[61]

Writing in 1922 in Germany just as that still quite new nation was engaged in its short-lived experiment with democratic rule, the great sociologist Max Weber famously explained the inevitability of this situation. As he laid it out in an oft-cited essay, democracy and the administrative state, or what he called bureaucracy, were destined to be at odds. They had, in fact, grown up and flourished in tandem. The logic of democracy, with its emphasis on the rational equalizing of privilege, just as much as the logic of capitalism, with its need for stable, predictable rules, required bureaucratic intervention along with the specialized, factual knowledge in which bureaucrats specialized. They depended upon one another. But because of the elitist and hierarchical rationale for the authority accorded to bureaucracy's corps of experts (*Fachbeamte* in his terms), as well as their independence from public judgments or even criticisms, the expansion of bureaucracy as both an institution and a way of thinking put it on a collision course with real democracy. That was, in fact, the key condition of modern politics. Bureaucrats were destined to become an interest group unto themselves and thus, over time, to undermine the exercise of popular sovereignty.[62]

Perhaps Weber got it right. (He did not live to see what happened to his own Weimar Republic.) The twentieth century certainly never shed the problem. Rather, it grew even in states that managed to remain democratic through the shocks of the two world wars and the pessimism about both democracy and capitalism characteristic of the period in between. Broadly speaking, reliance on expertise in the making of truth determinations has expanded exponentially through the twentieth century and into the twenty-first, though it is arguable whether it has done so to abet the expansion of capitalism on a global scale, to counter the social ills that capitalism inevitably creates, or some combination of both. What's sure is that ever more kinds and forms of data and information can be and are generated on more and more subjects. In part, this is thanks to new technological capacities. Computing power has quite obviously transformed what's possible at every level. In part, it's because of the ever-expanding needs of states for knowledge in new domains (think climate change, drug trafficking or dependency, maternal and children's health, educational achievement, housing costs, employment opportunities, drinking water standards, nuclear weapons manufacture, and on and on, nationally and for states around the world).

That also means more specialists in information than ever toil inside and out of government, some on the state's dime and some not. Fact-finders and researchers can be tracked down in ever more kinds of institutions, from a battalion of new government agencies to universities, industry research centers, political parties, NGOs, and "think tanks," some making projections about what will happen, but many just trying to establish what has already happened—Arendt's empirical truths—in the human and natural world. Today most developed societies boast full complements of consultants for consultants, advisors to advisors, spokespeople for other spokespeople, well exceeding anything Weber could have imagined. What these people share is generally a valuable commodity in our complex world: a specialized area of knowledge, training in a particular method or methods of data collection and analysis, and the ability to speak an often obscure but recognized jargon for conveying those findings that is viewed—especially in the elite circles to which these men and women already belong—as helpful in understanding all the noise around us. By now, every branch of the U.S. government even has its own corps of historians just to keep track of its own, internal history for the sake of policy-makers and the public alike.[63] Almost all state and federal agencies in the United States also have their own inspector-generals, primed for investigations into what has gone down, but also de facto underlining the importance of honesty in government in the first place (it is no surprise that most were instituted after the Watergate debacle).[64] And, of course, reporters and journalists of different stripes work hard to check on the veracity of all of this activity while also conveying basic findings back to a mass public.

For it has become something like a truism (even as more and more people distrust the government, especially in the United States) that the function of government is, as former President Obama frequently put it, "to get stuff done." States around the world now make foreign policy, defense policy, monetary policy, trade policy, tax policy, immigration policy, family policy, environmental policy, healthcare policy, labor policy, energy policy, science policy, education policy, even information policy (to borrow from the list put forth by political scientists Karen Orren and Stephen Skowronek).[65] Moreover, in the twentieth and into the twenty-first centuries, centralized, modernist "planning," anchored by the findings of large-scale demographic, economic, and scientific research, has ultimately been a feature of life in almost every kind of regime. That includes the Soviet Union and Fascist Italy and Japan, as well as capitalist democracies and their satellites. And while wars in the twentieth century seriously tested the resilience of democracy, "planning states" aimed at the rational, data-driven remaking of the existing world, or some part of it, have thrived in wartime and peacetime alike.

The achievements associated with all this policy-making and planning rooted in advances in the biological, physical, and social sciences should not be underestimated. Certain public initiatives of this sort, whether undertaken by international organizations like the United Nations and

World Health Organization or by national governments, have infiltrated daily lives in ways that have ended up benefiting large swathes of the world's population, including some of the most marginal of peoples. Public-health measures like inoculation campaigns, for example, or the provision of financial safety nets to society's most vulnerable, including the elderly (associated with the social democratic welfare state in Europe and considerably more minimally with the New Deal and then the Great Society in the United States), must be recognized as evidence of progress, to use an old-fashioned Enlightenment term.

Furthermore, expert knowledge has been vital to the resurgence of democracy as a form and an idea in the world outside the Soviet sphere in post-1945 Europe—and vice versa. In France, for example, in the aftermath of Nazi occupation and the Fascist Vichy regime, the question soon emerged of how best to revive that particular combination of liberal constitutionalism and self-rule that the French nation had once, back in the eighteenth century, helped to pioneer. French elites turned decisively to economic reform, or modernization projects, as the key, drawing on a long parallel tradition of centralized state planning dependent on experts at the helm that stretched back to the Third Republic, to Napoleon, to the Jacobins, even to the absolutist monarchy of Louis XIV. Economists, demographers, social workers, engineers, medical professionals, legal authorities: all were enlisted, via ministries and national institutes in the late 1940s and into the 1950s, to help buttress the family unit, ensure the public's health, oversee the state of schools and workplaces, rebuild infrastructure and housing, and, above all, modernize industry. French leaders took some pains, though, to get broad public buy-in (for advice *and* legitimacy), particularly when it came to the contours of the welfare state, and to expand the pool of "experts" to include women, Catholic charity professionals, trade unionists, and others who had previously been more likely to be left out. The "economic miracle" is the name often given now, along with *les Trente Glorieuses,* to the national resurgence that began in the Fourth Republic and continued, with even more powerful administrative and scientific elites in leadership roles, into the Fifth Republic and the presidency of Charles De Gaulle after 1958.[66] Certainly this was the tradition of expert-informed governance that the École Nationale d'Administration–educated Emmanuel Macron, seemingly taking a pointed jab at Trump, conjured up in a speech before the U.S. Congress when the leaders of the two nations met in Washington in April 2018: "I believe that against ignorance, we have education. Against inequalities, development. Against cynicism, trust and good faith. Against fanaticism, culture. Against disease and epidemics, medicine. Against the threats on the planet, science. I believe in concrete action. I believe the solutions are in our hands."[67]

But those inclined to see the scaling up of the hubris of Enlightenment thought in the twentieth century's "high modernist" planning efforts can point alternately to the apotheosis of technocracy—yet another neologism, this one of twentieth-century origins, meaning (now generally pejoratively) the rule of experts, and especially of economists and engineers, at the expense of the people and even politics.[68] They can also point to the spectacular failures technocratic planning efforts have also often brought in their wake.[69] Evidence comes first from colonial settings like Egypt and India, where undemocratic experts fixated on progress turned generalizations rooted in the West into seemingly universally applicable knowledge with often devastating effects, especially for peasants and their livelihoods and safety.[70] In mid-twentieth-century British East Africa, for example, "scientific agriculture" formed the basis of "total development schemes" that resulted in the building of new villages, the relocation of peoples, and the establishment of new land-tenure patterns that proved not only unpopular on the ground but also fundamentally ill-suited to local conditions and knowledge.[71] Still, in the aftermath of World War II, decolonization, and then the fall of the Berlin Wall, many of these policy-relevant techniques and assumptions gained a second life, as they were reappropriated for use in governance elsewhere—in the United States, in Latin America, and especially at home in Europe—as well as in newly independent postcolonial states. Democracy at its place of origin seems, in the late twentieth century, to have acquired an increasingly technocratic, "neoliberal" face.

Everyone's favorite example is the European Union (EU), created originally as the European Coal and Steel Community in 1951 (the same moment, more or less, as the French revival discussed above), to forge economic unity across Western Europe, but also to shore up democratic cooperation in the aftermath of World War II. To a real extent, it has worked. But since the 1950s, "Europe" has been steadily expanding its powers and range while also spawning an enormous, faceless bureaucracy and fostering extensive sets of new, supranational regulations. And for decades now, it has been widely attacked on both the left and the right for its "democratic deficit."[72] What is the charge? That the European Union, as it has been known since 1992, is ruled almost entirely by technocrats in Brussels, and everything happens very far from ordinary people, the "citizens" of Europe. More specifically, the standard complaint goes, the European people exercise little power over policy decisions, especially since the meat and potatoes of the whole operation is the unelected European Commission in Brussels; they have almost no means to hold anyone accountable once decisions do get taken; there is little transparency anyway, since most of the work happens behind closed doors; and even what does get reported is rarely intelligible since it typically results in a bonanza of jargon, charts, reports, and ultimately rulings that few have the knowledge or tenacity to tackle. Jean Monnet might have imagined at mid-century some smooth-operating system he called *engrenage,* but decision-making is actually now bogged down in negotiations between endless working groups, regulatory bodies, and committees of technical experts from industry and the civil service alike, forming what is sometimes called a "closed epistemic community." No wonder the EU is often described as hard to love!

None of that, though, really sounds so unusual today. It is how government works almost everywhere. As the English political scientist John Dunn points out, quite sensibly, democracy now means really only that the state draws its legitimacy from us, not that we *actually* rule ourselves.[73] Certainly, in many places in the world these days, a good part of the population has been effectively disenfranchised by one means or another from part or all of policy-making (think, for example, of nondemocratic institutions like central banks setting monetary policy unilaterally, or think of nationally based citizenship and age requirements for voters all over the world). Those eligible to vote cannot be counted on to do so either, apart from in places like Australia and Argentina with compulsory suffrage. That's a result of lack of engagement, which usually gets pegged as apathy. That's also because it can often seem as if, in today's mass society, the act of voting hardly matters in any concrete way. Traditional political parties have been losing voters in both the United States and Europe.[74]

But there is more: European citizens have, in recent decades, often expressed the sentiment that the EU's actions themselves are in no way responsive to ordinary people's needs, interests, or even lived experiences (an opinion that many Americans living "outside the Beltway" evince about Washington too). British fishermen have been particularly vocal on this front, complaining that lack of attention to their local needs and habits has resulted in regulations that have simultaneously deprived them of their livelihood (when not turning fishing into a criminal activity) *and* devastated vital fishing grounds, especially on the continental shelf around the United Kingdom.[75] The only people who have benefitted from EU policies, according to many ordinary Europeans, are global elites, the kinds of people who value the interests of big business and "efficiency" over social justice and redistribution (in the left-wing critique) and over national interest (in the right-wing one). The result is something like liberalism without democracy, or technical, business-friendly solutions to governance determined by economists and bankers, rather than the messy democratic way to truth. For just as Weber foresaw, this pulling away of experts, ensconced in their bureaucratic strongholds and convinced of their own authority, poses some serious problems for the long-term health of the polity.

The first is simply bad policy. Fatal errors in judgment can result from the "bubble effect" of educated elites isolating themselves from ordinary people and closing ranks in what John Stuart Mill once called mockingly a pedantocracy and others since have called an epistocracy, expertocracy, or, recently, liberalocracy.[76] That can be the case whether it stems from experts' self-regard in light of their ostensibly superior knowledge or from their being deep in the pockets of other kinds of oligarchical powers, from entrenched politicians to captains of industry. Or, to put it slightly differently, we can and do end up with faulty determinations and then faulty government programs both as a result of insiders lying to the public (ordinary deception) and as a result of insiders lying to themselves (self-deception).

When experts talk exclusively among themselves, barricading themselves off from the public and, it follows, the public from the business of democratic judgments, they potentially lose a lot cognitively, especially when the corps of experts is socially or intellectually homogeneous to begin with, as has traditionally been the case. They forfeit helpful oversight. They forego the opportunity to hear criticism and countervailing takes, whether from inside their own ranks or outside. Most of all, they pass up the opportunity to benefit from local, situated institutions and knowledge—for example, what fishermen in the ports of Hull or Aberdeen say about the conditions in U.K. waters right now, which amounts to the truth according to people who understand these issues in an experiential rather than scientific way. (Classic examples of the dangers of ignoring local knowledge usually involve male experts failing to consult women in developing nations on water issues and only later discovering that all their technical efforts are doomed as a result of not having taken into account or even heard about these women's daily experiences as providers for their families or the place of water in local customs and history.)[77] Furthermore, in such circumstances, experts can easily not recognize their *own* biases (Isn't greed or the quest for status, for example, just as much an emotional motivation as often-disparaged popular resentments and fears? Isn't a probusiness position ideological too?). Or experts can grow complacent, even overconfident, and think they have all the answers and are infallible. Or they can simply believe their own propaganda and mistake it for proof.

This is just what Arendt thought had happened in the buildup to the *Pentagon Papers*. "Spin" or public relations–style massaging of information so as to deceive the public was not, she claimed, the only fresh form of lying to emerge in the political world of the early 1970s. Arendt also drew readers' attention to what she took to be the historically novel type of lying characteristic of the modern, self-deceiving technocrat, who starts with the theory and makes the facts fit accordingly precisely because he is so convinced of his own rightness and expertise. Living in what has actually become a "defactualized world," the technocrat lies out of a sense of duty to uphold the images of the world that are already in place.[78] With all his numbers and percentages, he still cannot see his way outside the propaganda that he has helped construct.[79] And such risks of going analytically astray typically only get magnified (say yet another corps of experts today) when experts who are cut off from popular perceptions or alternative voices use their knowledge of the past to make predictions or to plan ahead, another part of many bureaucrats' job descriptions.[80] Objective knowledge on which good policy can be built can be harder to find than it looks.

These days, though, experts may not even think of themselves as neutral fact-providers or devisers of apolitical technical solutions. Since the 1970s, a good number of U.S. political "experts" have, in fact, worked for unabashedly right-leaning or left-leaning think tanks like the Heritage Foundation (founded 1973), the Cato Institute (1977), or Human Rights Watch (1978), which receive most of their funding from corporate and individual donors and essentially issue reports designed to help lawmakers on their own side market their latest policy ideas. This is the case in the United Kingdom too. The research arms of the major political parties do something similar. Even venerable and ostensibly neutral, nonpartisan think tanks like the Brookings Institution in Washington, we now know thanks to recent exposés, are frequently bought by corporate and other special interests eager to trade on their imprimatur. The *New York Times* reported in 2016 on the common practice at such institutions of not only the lending of expert credentials to paying industry professionals, but also the creation of for-pay "research" that spins truth in just such a way as to ultimately line the pockets of the fat cats covering the bills.[81]

At the same time, a seemingly revolving door allows various kinds of political professionals and experts to travel repeatedly and almost seamlessly from academia, to government agencies or legislative bodies, to industry (including its lobbying arms), and back again, while government fact-finding agencies like the Environmental

Protection Agency or the Food and Drug Administration are themselves awash in interest-group and corporate money. In the United States, the deregulation of campaign finance in recent years has hardly helped matters either, since it has brought an infusion of ever more money, not all of it easily traceable, into every election cycle. Wealthy private donors, corporations, and other groups can now use cash to tailor or manipulate information, limit choices, or twist the questions, thereby shaping election results. They can also "buy" elected officials directly. What that ultimately means is that old—and some would argue, outdated—boundaries between expert research and advocacy, objective facts and advertising, suasion and outright purchasing, have increasingly disappeared, and policy has less and less to do with the democratic will—even if it isn't presented that way. Is it any wonder that many people look at politics at the national level, with its talking heads and pundits and their competing data and studies, and see nothing but a display of hypocrisy and corruption?

Yet even this might not be the worst of it. Technocratic expertise can, finally, threaten the basic values of equality, pluralism, and shared decision-making on which democracy is meant to stand. Now, ideally, in moments when experts overstep their authority too blatantly, civil society swings into action, resisting technocratic excess in an effort to restore some balance. Ordinary people, local organizations, the press: while they might continue to look, as needed, to uncompromised "scientific" experts as aids, even teachers, in the world of public policy options, they also work to add their own truths to the mix, and they make sure never to relinquish their democratic role as the primary decision-makers. This might be described as the

Deweyan ideal. However, when technocracy grows too extensive and entrenched and starts to take up all the political oxygen, other outcomes present themselves as possibilities. If ordinary people feel disenfranchised (formally or informally) for too long, and civil society grows weak and apathetic as a result, the way can also open for technocrats, in conjunction with long-serving "professional politicians" as insider experts in their own right and possibly business elites, to do more than ignore ordinary people's conceptions of and desires for the world or mislead them about their options. Such managerial elites can also start exercising power more directly, turning increasingly authoritarian and dogmatic about the truth in the process. This is what Arendt meant when she (rather perversely) declared that truth *can* have a "despotic" character, taking politics beyond the realm of dispute into manufactured consent.[82]

Yet the opposite result is just as possible. Alternately, a substantial number of those same ordinary people can, in response to long-simmering resentment, gradually stop putting any stock in expert voices of any kind, seeing all of them as hacks or phonies speaking only for themselves and their partisan, financially interested cronies. That's when facts start to look indistinguishable from opinions or beliefs, the former appearing as just a disguised manifestation of the latter. That's also when the way becomes clear for a demagogic outsider who, with the help of alternative media like far right news sources that spring up to aid the process with conspiracy theories and vituperation directed against enemies, promises to elevate "the people" over all sources of knowledge, from universities to major newspapers to beholden politicians, who can be said to be complicit in elite, technocratic rule.

This, in a nutshell, is what has happened in much of the world as of late. If technocracy attached to global capitalism has increasingly threatened to overpower the ideal of cooperative democratic decision-making in the modern, postrevolutionary world (all the while heightening inequalities in the process), the reaction, with its characteristic anger and know-nothingness, has started to constitute its own form of risk. With deep roots, but big growth spurts in the 1980s and again in the last few years, an anti-expert ethos has now resulted in an assault on truth in two senses: as a form of factuality rooted in specific institutions, methods, and training, and as an ethical position. That danger, in its historical context, is the subject of the next chapter.

The Populist Reaction

Long before anyone started talking about "technocracy," a backlash began—a backlash against the idea of an elite that holds a monopoly on truth, a backlash against the idea of any small group of citizens or subjects requiring epistemic deference on the part of everyone else. The reaction started before the Age of Revolutions. Resentment at such notions actually helped spur quasi-democratic uprisings in the eighteenth and early nineteenth centuries. And the reaction has continued long after, especially among those who have taken literally the language of popular sovereignty and the idea that the real rulers—and knowers—are "the people."[1]

At its best, this defense of the wisdom and will of the *demos* has been a means to justify all sorts of social and political movements directed toward securing equality and dignity for those traditionally denied it. Over the centuries, it has been deployed by urban artisans and industrial workers in Genoa, Marseille, and other European cities; by slave rebels in the Caribbean; by anticaste agitators in India; and by women everywhere.[2] Rights talk, combined with the idea of the nation, has, perhaps, been the most visible weapon in global struggles for justice, as rebels have often made their primary demand a "right" to be seen and heard, whether in the public sphere or the hustings (which has also meant that economic demands have often taken a back seat). But major social and political movements have also necessarily built on the moral-epistemic notion that all humans have the capacity—individually and, even more, collectively—to tell true from false, right from wrong, the core of political judgment. Even more, they have insisted that the realm of politics is perfectly suited to these capacities insofar as politics should be primarily about determining and conveying basic truths derived from life experience or what has come to be known as common sense.

The English Dissenter and schoolmaster James Burgh made the case well before the American Revolutionary War, picking up an old theme in radical English politics and religious life: politics was a realm in which no one really has any claims to superiority. There was little reason to believe that "the brain of a statesman [was] made of materials different from that of a citizen" *or* that one had to be "a master of sublime geometry . . . to judge of political subjects." On the contrary, all that was needed to participate in politics was "plain sense, applied to *general,* instead of private concerns" and "common honesty"—the stock of almost everyone alive.[3] A hundred years later, in the thick of the debate on universal manhood suffrage, John Stuart Mill was still repeating basically the same point, albeit always with caveats about "barbarians" in far-off lands that suggests the way bias always infiltrates such discussions: "I do not say that the [English] working men's view of those questions is in general nearer to truth than the other: but it is sometimes quite as near; and in any case ought to be respectfully listened to" when it came to circumstances that would affect them.[4]

This old defense of the basic capacity of nonelites to help generate political truth has also, at various moments, been taken one step further. Radicals have, for several centuries, drawn on a long, predemocratic tradition of "inverse inegalitarianism"—the recognition of the superiority in certain regards of those looked-down-upon *over* their social betters—to make the case for expanding the definition and authority of "the people."[5] By this logic, those who have long been excluded from the political body are ultimately "nearer to truth" (in Mill's words), and consequently more trustworthy, in two important senses. Ordinary or overlooked people can be said to be more honest, meaning considerably less liable to lie or obfuscate or fudge or mislead than self-interested elites trying to look like what they are not. We might tag them straight-shooters today. Ordinary or overlooked people can also, in epistemic terms, be said to see the world they inhabit much more clearly in the first place than either fat cats who can't tell you the price of milk or head-in-the-clouds intellectuals who sit in their ivory towers pondering esoteric problems in esoteric terms.

This advantage could be a function of their very "nature." As a woman, claimed the French feminist revolutionary Olympe de Gouges, she possessed a special connection to a long-lost "tutelary angel" called good sense that her male counterparts, whether clerics, savants, nobles, or political types, uniformly lacked.[6] Or it could be because their lowly social position had, as an unforeseen benefit, left them uncorrupted by formal education and books, and thus considerably more grounded, as many a text ostensibly penned by an eighteenth- or nineteenth-century "old man of good sense" or "plain farmer" or just "one of the people" claimed.[7] Or, by the twentieth century, it could be explained as a consequence of their alternative subjectivities, the idea that truth looks different depending on just where you stand and gaze out at the world.

Today, "epistemic democrats" argue something not altogether different: that when it comes to politics, ordinary people, collectively, have their own kind of expertise—and it often generates better outcomes in terms of knowledge than does that of a rarified cohort of official experts. This idea echoes very clearly Aristotle's qualified claims for the wisdom of the many over the few, as well as old Christian notions like "*vox populi, vox dei.*" But it also turns on its head a traditional argument about the weakness of democracy, which says that though self-rule might be good for achieving equity, liberty, fairness, or some other abstract principle, it is less good for its practical results. That is because it leaves consequential decisions at the mercy of the people's ignorance, impracticality, and volatile emotions. The alternative claim of epistemic democrats, is, simply put, that democratic decision-making can and should be defended expressly as knowledge-producing.[8] According to these contemporary psychologists and political theorists, when a group of people is sufficiently informed, diverse in perspective, and attentive to lay knowledge that might otherwise not be on recognized experts' radar screens, that group will arrive at objectively superior or more correct judgments than a team of technocrats. Each member of the crowd will contribute his or her own bit of knowledge, discerned primarily through personal, on-the-ground experience, and the collectivization of this knowledge through democratic processes, or something like "crowdsourcing," will move us closer to what some of these theorists call political truth.[9]

Epistemic democrats make this case with a lot of empirical research, in most cases seemingly oblivious to the irony of university-based experts using social science data to prove that the untutored people, with their alternative methods, actually know best. But a related logic actually already buttresses, more informally, a set of older, predemocratic political institutions. The jury, a traditional royal mechanism for determining the truth or falsity of claims in legal cases, constitutes one key example. Starting in the mid-thirteenth century, English courts began depending upon juries to pool the mental powers of a varied group of local people. They have done so ever since to serve both an evolving epistemological function (as courts have over time become more invested in fact-finding) and a moral one, including shifting the weighty responsibility for judging truth from any one individual to a group.[10] Traditionally, holding local knowledge, including knowing the people involved at least by reputation, was a plus. By the eighteenth century, it was also sometimes argued (as in cases of seditious libel) that it was precisely because ordinary people naturally make inferences from facts based on "common sense" rather than "technical learning" that institutions like juries, which depend upon the collective cognitive powers of ordinary people, were so useful.[11] (That same dependence on regular folks, in all their unpredictability and variability, is also the primary reason that technocrats in the early twentieth century, including the inventors of the polygraph, once hoped to render the jury obsolete.)[12]

A related logic has also long governed the history of voting, which predates the Age of Revolutions as well. From ancient Greece to Renaissance Venice to early modern French municipalities, elections functioned not just as ceremonies of legitimation. They were also designed as mechanisms to help heterogeneous groups make good, collective, and often consensual decisions rooted in their sense of the world—and without resorting to violence.[13] Elections, like courts, generated communal determinations. This remains, like the reasoning behind juries, a solid argument for the classic democratic approach to truth outlined in chapter 1—and, indeed, for its expansion to include an ever wider set of voices in the business of democracy. It is, after all, only in the last century that either of these institutions became fully open in the United States to people of color or women, and many categories of persons, including felons, adolescents under age eighteen, and noncitizens, remain excluded in various places to this day.

The pushback to the idea of a small caste of experts who function as authorities in truth has, however, never been solely about involving a more diverse array of peoples in political decision-making or enhancing cooperation between political elites and "the people" as truth-seekers. Sometimes quite different logic has prevailed. By the start of the nineteenth and increasingly through the twentieth and into the twenty-first centuries, it also became very possible to argue for "the people" alone, or "the people" and a single trustworthy leader dedicated to their cause, as the primary or even sole source of truth in a democracy—and for the wholesale rejection of experts and their expert knowledge, as well as other outlying sources of information, as having little valuable to contribute besides partisanship and error. What's interesting is that this case has depended on calling public attention to the same enduring gap as have liberation movements: between the high ideals associated with popular sovereignty, liberty, and equality, on the one hand, and on the other, the nasty, messy reality of both democratic and capitalist practice, in which nonelites are often pushed to the margins and inequality reigns on every front.

The key is that "the people" (or *le peuple, das Volk,* or any other cognate) is a complicated, ambiguous construct in the modern world. It is also always up for grabs. And as a means to stimulate protest, it can be—and is—as easily defined as homogenous and monolithic as it is varied and pluralist. Think of the evocation of certain broad sociological categorizations like "Christian people" or, even more, of moral and epistemic ones (which often end up dovetailing with or papering over sociological ones, including "white people") like "patriotic people," "virtuous people," "sensible people," "ordinary people," "hardworking people," "authentic people," or even *the* people. What these categories have in common, despite their slipperiness, is that they all imply the existence of a mass of individuals who already all agree with one another about what's right versus wrong or true versus false and don't need any fancy procedures or dialectics, political or otherwise, to get there.[14] That also means the essential democratic concept of "the people" can be used not only as a tool for increasing inclusion. It can also be a way to produce new kinds of exclusions and, indeed, the kind of social and political polarization and tribalism we are witnessing today. For one great temptation is to see outliers—typically well-off, over-educated elites and, in more right-wing versions, elites' marginal allies as well—not as potential partners in a common pursuit but, rather, as standing in the way of the realization of both democracy and its promise to deliver the truth.

Populism is, of course, much in the news these days. What it is not is an ideology or a fixed program. Rather, it is best described as a style or logic or, I am going to suggest, narrative framework for conceptualizing and shaping political power that builds on the assumed opposition between these two starkly defined camps.[15] Typically, it begins with a (self-congratulatory) exaltation of the *real* people, the unjustifiably powerless. It adds a gripe about the past that often morphs into a full-blown conspiracy theory starring the unjustifiably powerful. It concludes with a fairytale-like denouement and a new, mythic social role for its adherents. What is less noticed is how much it—like Progressives' arguments for the enhancement of expert guidance, which flourished at much the same moment in the late nineteenth century—depends upon a set of suppositions about how and where truths to live by, or validated beliefs, are to be found in a real democracy. Only in this case, the solution involves rejecting ostensibly objective expertise and all the institutions, values, norms, procedures, and people that expertise goes with and valorizing a combination of quotidian experience and the feelings, impulses, beliefs, and intuitions of ordinary people instead.[16]

The critical and essential claim at the heart of any populist politics is that the (plain, ordinary, hardworking, silent—your choice!) people in the majority know best *and* are the most virtuous. They collectively have a kind of instinctual, practical knowledge of the world that is particularly suited to the political sphere (as opposed to, say, the more arcane world of the science lab), and they are sincere and authentic in ways that make them incapable of engaging in deception when it comes to delivering this knowledge to others. Indeed, the idea that, once upon a time, the real people had, or should have had, a large voice in political life, especially since they are, in principle, sovereign, can itself be considered a lost truth that must be reclaimed. (Nostalgia is often a big part of populism, as in "make America great *again*.")

However, in the standard populist narrative, the key discovery—the one that will now change the game and produce a new political identity for adherents—is that the people have been betrayed by the very individuals in whom they had put their trust.[17] The opportunity to define the world by naming its truths has been hijacked by unspecified elites, including technocrats, plutocrats, journalists, foreigners, elected officials, and intellectuals in a world in which power, money, and intellectual clout tend to go together. While these people might look and act like independent brokers of truth and demand the confidence of others based on their institutional credentials or their wealth, they are actually partisan, self-interested, and corrupt as they try hard to defend an indefensible status quo (an accusation which, as we've seen, is sometimes true, but is often a mythology unto itself). Moreover, these same exploitative elites are often described as being in cahoots with various downtrodden or marginal groups, like immigrants or Jews or welfare recipients or members of a particular racial minority, all of whom can be said not to belong to the "real" people either. The conspiracy is the hidden, nefarious process by which all these "enemies of the people" have, over time, substituted their self-serving and ultimately false way of perceiving and talking about the world—their phony truths—for the people's practical, instinctive beliefs and thereby left the whole society at a deep disadvantage.

The populist storyline, though, comes with a ready solution to this epistemological and political crisis. Populism, as a way of thinking about and narrating the fate of truth and power, demands two basic corrective actions: revelation—or exposing the conspiracy—and restoration of a better, more just status quo. First, the ordinary (or virtuous or authentic) people need to open their eyes to the now-revealed, actual truth and name their enemies honestly (i.e., the "dishonest media"). Then, these same people must throw out all the fancy-pants, obscurantist, deliberately misleading methods, jargon, and personnel emanating from Cambridge, Massachusetts, or Washington, D.C., or London, or Brussels (i.e., "drain the swamp") and substitute officials and media spokespeople who are truly representative of the people. That means those who are willing to tell it like it *really* is—with candor, in simple language, and rooted in everyday experience and, often, intuition or faith—and make policy, if necessary, accordingly. That, or get rid of all intermediaries and their arcane processes altogether. Then real democracy can prevail once again, with "the people" truly calling the shots.

For the payoff promises to be extraordinary—and more than simply a matter of justice. Under these conditions, the conflict-ridden politics of the moment will essentially cease. In place of debate and dissension, populists typically suggest a coming world of consensus and of simple, practical, even obvious, nonideological fixes, should the right people prevail. This isn't a world without any commitment to objective truth or reality (the analogy with postmodernist conceptions of truth is entirely wrong on this front). Rather, this is, in many respects, the exact inverted image of the world imagined by technocrats: a world in which truth does not require complex, cooperative procedures involving negotiations between multiple parties with divergent views, but simply the natural problem-solving faculties of a subset of the population that actually knows better. Populists get there differently; they tend to reject science and its methods as a source of directives, embracing in many cases emotional honesty, intuition, and truths of the heart over dry factual veracity and scientific evidence, testing, and credentialing. They also embrace a different style of expression. However, they share with technocrats a distaste for politics as agonistic tussling with a vocal opposition and, ultimately, when pushed too far, the democratic recipe to truth production with its roots in the Founding Era.

That's the bare outlines of the populist logic. To find out how this perennial narrative and its claims came to exist, we need to step back one final time into the Enlightenment, the intellectual culture in which modern democracy was born. Yes, as noted in the previous chapter, "the public sphere" and "public opinion" were elite notions from the beginning, attached both in practice and in aspiration to an enlightened class. Furthermore, to this day the history of the Enlightenment remains more often tied to the nineteenth-century idea of the "expert" and the pursuit of rational truth associated with these new elites than to the populist currents with which it long competed. Yet two essential features of modern populist epistemology trace their roots very much to the world of Kant, Voltaire, de Gouges, and Jefferson: the instrumental, political use of the idea of the wisdom of the common person and a taste for critique and exposure that easily veers into conspiracy theorizing.

The *philosophe* may not, as we've seen, naturally have been any kind of good friend to the common, uneducated man (or woman) of the eighteenth century. But clever, upstart writers of that era quickly discovered that to challenge the power and pervasiveness of received wisdom, they could claim to stand with the plain, simple people—especially those who could be described as closer to nature and untainted by corrupt, overcivilized ways—against the establishment and its emissaries, be they priests or lords or stodgy Harvard or Oxbridge professors. Reason, but even more common sense, the idea of a kind of instinctive knowledge born of ordinary men's day-to-day experience and highly effective in cutting through platitudes of all kinds, was reinvented in the aftermath of the Glorious Revolution for just this purpose. Dissenting Protestantism and other nonorthodox religious traditions gave this idea of the instinctive, self-generated knowledge of regular folks a further boost. Here, ripe for philosophic, then political repurposing (though not necessarily from the ground up) was an alternative form of epistemic authority to that of aristocrats, divines, savants, kings, and all other spokesmen for orthodoxy or dogmatic truth. Plus, it followed directly from the key Enlightenment principle that what is simple and clear and closer to nature must always trump that which is complex, intricate, and mysterious (often described as "scholastic" or "baroque" to evoke the corrupt past) in any crusade to eradicate prejudice and error. Before the first of the eighteenth-century revolutions, this notion of the people's infallible, experiential wisdom had been put to use by English journalists challenging "ministerial despotism," Scottish philosophers and clerics attempting to stifle a dangerous skepticism that tested the idea of God, and exiled French writers in the radical Dutch underground who wanted to undercut hypocritical Catholic moral and sexual values any way that they could. As such, the legitimating myth of the common people, endowed with a common, quotidian wisdom that surpassed in veracity the highfalutin logic and rhetoric of elites, was actually born right alongside its opposite, the myth of the holders of exceptional knowledge as a social caste defined by its vital public function.[18]

Conspiracy thinking has deep Enlightenment roots as well. It too might seem atavistic, a relic of the premodern world, when secrecy was, by design, the operative principle of government, and news and rumor could frequently not be told apart. But the Enlightenment taste for peering behind curtains and doors and exposing bad faith to bright light fueled a publishing industry (underground in much of Europe while censors prowled) that thrived on revelations of nefarious doings, the real truth from behind the veil. How else to explain all the books and pamphlets and journals with titles like *The English Spy: Secret Correspondence between Milord All' Eye and Milord All' Ear,* a purported cache of recovered letters that turned the tables on a secretive French state and made the reader into both eavesdropper and voyeur?[19]

And while the radical transparency promised by the advent of republics might seem logically as if it should have put an end to the need for such practices, the culture of conspiracy only grew in the transatlantic Age of Revolutions.[20] Partly the destabilization of the norms of daily life and uncertainty about the future encouraged wild theories to explain what was happening. Under conditions of extreme precariousness, trust is hard to come by, and even facts seem open to reappraisal. But just as much, the explosion of the press that followed the deregulation of speech, combined with a burgeoning capitalist marketplace, helped create a context whereby rumor and "fake news" could flourish as easily as truth. Conspiracy theories proved popular with readers, who could thus locate themselves on the side of the savvy. That meant conspiracy theories also turned moneymaking for their inventors in the world of print. Moreover, in the context of the French Revolution, the collision of the enlightened idea of total publicity with the reality of unstoppable counter-revolutionary activity produced constant fear—or, really, paranoia—that what was being witnessed on the surface was not the whole truth, that some other truth (disloyalty, for example) lay hidden out of view. Such anxieties fueled the punitive culture of the Terror, with its reliance on forced unmasking, jail terms, and guillotines, and then eventually brought it—and its chief architect, Robespierre—crashing down as well. For as the French discovered at the height of the Terror, no amount of counterevidence or counterargument could make much traction against all these stories of plotting and subterfuge; the naysayer ended up looking like a dupe himself or, worse, complicit in it all.

Both trends—the weaponized exaltation of the common man's wisdom and the flourishing of conspiracy thinking—then contributed not only to the undoing of the Old Regime's "despotic" monarchies in the course of the eighteenth and nineteenth centuries, but also to the solidification and, ultimately, victory of democracy, understood as largely dependent on the significance of the people's truth. Thomas Paine is only the most famous example of how these currents worked together, at the level of narrative, to motivate an ambivalent public. Much of his celebrated and highly effective political pamphlet *Common Sense* (1776) was given over to tales of "the people" of America being tricked and deceived, forced to swallow unwittingly all kinds of logic on the part of the British ruling classes that actually ran contrary to the people's basic understanding of the world. Was there not, for example, "something absurd, in supposing a continent to be perpetually governed by an island"?[21] But Paine also promised that the people held within themselves the power to right this ship. Finally throwing off aristocracy and monarchy once and for all would make it possible to institute a kind of government in which the people's common sense really did rule the day, figuratively and literally. Furthermore, he pushed all this in an idiom rife with biblical references, homespun wisdom, and blunt, sometimes overwrought emotional force. Paine's goal was to twist the arms of ordinary folks to accept a currently unpopular message, but also to suggest that the author himself was but the people's tribune, quite the opposite of the learned, stilted, and distant authorities (British and colonial) whose views he was so eager to topple. That contradiction aside, Paine's *Common Sense* thus became an object lesson in the kind of no-compromise, Manichean populist discourse that helped set modern democracy, in the guise of the republic, in motion. In short, it worked.

No wonder his example found imitators among subsequent revolutionaries well into the nineteenth century, from Paris to Hamburg to Lima.[22]

Our story does not stop there, however—not by a longshot. That's because once republics were up and running, populist epistemology in the mold of Paine also quickly helped produce and feed the emergence of an oppositional culture, this time directed *against* these republics' new political and intellectual leadership class. Significantly, that happened on both the right and the left, themselves new political designations of the 1790s. It also came from above as well as below. What took off with the protest politics of anti-Federalists, radical Jacobins, and counterrevolutionaries of all stripes has lasted to this day, strengthening and undermining democracy at the same time.

The U.S. Constitution, with its lofty prose, careful commitment to checks and balances, and antimajoritarian thrust, spawned a cottage industry challenging its legitimacy before the ink of the text was even dry. Many of the counterarguments were, and remain, convincing. For critics rightly detected in the late 1780s that this document was ultimately undemocratic in its details (just as its framers intended) and would help institute if not a hereditary elite in the British mold, then a political ruling class, or new form of "aristocracy" as it was usually dubbed, nevertheless. Indeed, the Constitution's adversaries insisted that the whole thing smelled of Old World corruption: a wealthy, educated faction conspiring to empower itself at the expense of the plebs through a kind of sleight-of-hand. Amos Singletary, an anti-Federalist delegate to the Massachusetts ratifying constitution, insisted that the new Constitution was the work of an intellectual cabal: "lawyers, men of learning, and moneyed men, that talk so finely, and gloss over matters so smoothly, to make us poor illiterate people swallow down the pill" before they then "swallow up all us little folks."[23] The Philadelphia essayist calling himself Centinel (probably George Bryan) railed more grandiloquently in the pages of the *Independent Gazette* in 1788 against the "Machiavellian talents, of those who excel in ingenuity, artifice, sophistry, and the refinements of falsehood, who can assume the pleasing appearance of truth and bewilder the people in all the mazes of error," as well as men of "great learning, eloquence and sophistry . . . disposed to delude by deceptive glosses and specious reasoning."[24] Dishonesty and deception, via obfuscation and other language crimes, became the standard charge. John Adams noted some years later that learning and virtue did not necessarily have to go together, that the former was available to "knaves and hypocrites . . . as well as honest, candid, and sincere men."[25] His opponents at the end of the eighteenth century proposed that, in practice, they rarely did.

But what to do? Anti-Federalists jumped on an argument that was already present at the moment of the writing of the first state constitutions starting in 1776: that the time had arrived to institute something that looked more like the rule of the people, that is, to realize the true leveling spirit of democracy. What was needed were legislators who perceived and experienced the world in the terms of ordinary men. To this end, anti-Federalist propagandists began by turning what had been the badges of the commoner's inferiority, including his poor language and lack of erudition, into signs of superiority—and denigrating the educated and well-connected as tainted by the culture

of academic obscurantism and "European" (read: cosmopolitan) insincerity in which they were steeped (all to the
dismay of men like the émigré architect Benjamin Latrobe,
who worried that the leveling spirit had succeeded to such
a degree that "men of talents" now actually excited distrust
in the political sphere). As the progressive Vermonter Samuel Williams bluntly insisted in 1794, "The public opinion
will be much nearer the truth, than the reasonings and
refinements of speculative or interested men."[26]

At almost the same moment, radical revolutionaries in
France, along with their supporters in England and on the
Continent, made a similar case for the honesty and clear-
sightedness of ordinary men, especially in the aggregate,
in contrast to compromised elites. Bad spelling and poor
grammar on the part of any number of men and women of
good sense (or often *le gros bon sens, le bon sens populaire,
or le bon sens villageoise*) offering their take on the events
of the day was now held up as evidence of trustworthi-
ness. Here, straight from their eyes to the page, was the
unvarnished, unadulterated expression of truth. The very
authority of authors like one calling herself "a patriotic
woman" (*une femme patriote*) stemmed from their distance from the traditional centers of language and power.[27]
The contrast with the contemporaneous 1793 French Law
of Suspects, which detailed a long list of language crimes
by which "suspected persons" could be said to be duping
a credulous public, is telling. What this emergency law
warned French citizens to be on the lookout for was less
those who went around explicitly expressing counter-
revolutionary ideas than those who knew how to commit
sophisticated forms of linguistic fraud, including those
who arrest the energy of public assemblies through "crafty

discourses, turbulent cries and threats," those who "speak mysteriously of the misfortunes of the republic . . . always ready to spread bad news with an affected grief," and those who "have the words *liberté, égalité, république,* and *patrie* constantly on their lips, but . . . consort with former nobles, counterrevolutionary priests, aristocrats . . . [and] moderates, and show concern for their fate."[28]

What is perhaps more surprising is that a variant of this argument about the genuine as opposed to misleading sources of truth in public life took shape at the same time on the emergent political right. It began with Edmund Burke's seminal 1790 attack on the foundational principles of the French Revolution. Opponents of radical revolutionary principles certainly reaffirmed from the start the importance of hierarchy and deference in the world of ideas, as in all other spheres. Indeed, they recoiled almost immediately, as might be expected, at the rise of obscure men without name or distinction taking on leadership roles in local governments and at the national level. But across the Channel, Burke tried out another argument in his path-breaking *Reflections on the Revolution in France:* that the greatest danger emanating from that nation was less the demands of the people themselves than the burgeoning taste for the values of "sophisters, economists, and calculators," the precursors to the nineteenth century's experts. As he explained it, the new political class post-1789 was, perversely, made up of men who "despise experience as the wisdom of unlettered men" (farmers and doctors are his chief examples of those currently being ignored) and instead attach themselves to the "political metaphysics" and "abstract rule" favored by professor-types. Nothing could be more of a mistake. For when it came to where truth should be found, "the pretended rights of these theorists are all extremes; and in proportion as they are metaphysically true, they are morally and politically false."[29]

Burke's insight—that revolutions about rights, citizenship, and national sovereignty turned on abstractions that had little reality in the lives of ordinary people concerned fundamentally with questions like the price of bread—became a constant theme of Catholic counterrevolutionaries attacking Robespierre and his allies in France, as well as anti-Jeffersonians in the new United States. In both cases, the accusation was that national leadership had been captured by a speculative system-builder, a man who simply made things up in his head (including the very idea of a revolution in the name of intangible ideals like equality) and failed to follow basic empirical evidence as sensible people of all walks of life, including women and peasants steeped in tradition and local know-how, did. As the American historian Richard Hofstadter pointed out many decades ago in his famous chronicle of two centuries of American anti-intellectualism (though without pointing out the contradiction that the progenitors of this discourse were typically highly educated men themselves), Jefferson's original sin was widely understood circa 1800 to be his attachment to Enlightenment-style philosophizing. The Massachusetts Congressman Fisher Ames claimed Jefferson had been "carried away by systems, and the everlasting zeal to generalize, instead of proceeding, like common men of practical sense, on the low, but sure foundation of matter of fact." Others insisted that Jefferson was caught up with meaningless abstractions rather than "the existing state of things and circumstances."[30] Such charges were meant to undermine Jefferson's authority but also the democratic stance on truth more generally. What's interesting is that opponents of the republican revolution from both sides, albeit for different reasons, came back to the idea that *only* common sense, intuition, and "experience"—the latter understood not as book learning or erudition, but as what Burke also called "practical wisdom"—and their progenitors could be the proper sources for legitimate truth.

And just as with expertise, this populist understanding of truth, in both its right- and left-wing incarnations, grew all over the Atlantic world in the nineteenth and into the twentieth centuries, sometimes as a threat to democracy and sometimes as a constituent element of it. Resentment concerning a world structured around economic inequality was one source of its ongoing popularity. As equality (or its promise) gradually expanded on certain fronts, including suffrage and access to education, ever-greater economic differentiation took off as its steady counterpart in the age of industrial capitalism. The language of the people's common sense became a vehicle for fighting back against condescension, snobbery, and expectations of deference on the part of those who possessed the refinements tied to money above all else in an era of mass politics. It also helped ordinary people voice a healthy skepticism about official truth claims and challenge their overly dogmatic qualities, unmasking them as covers for naked self-interest. But as in the case of Fisher Ames, the appeal to the wisdom of the people was always used as much by wealthy politicians, industry leaders, and intellectuals, all claiming to speak for the masses and to defend them from other undemocratic elites, as it was by veritable ordinary people. It also blended when needed (just as the discourse of expertise did) with just about every important ideology of the era, including nationalism and socialism. As the historian Patrick Joyce points out in regard to nineteenth-century England, populism pervaded the full spectrum of popular politics, sometimes as a way of drawing voters, sometimes as a way of explaining policy, and always closely linked to pandering.[31]

In the end, a burgeoning postrevolutionary, populist epistemology had a substantial effect on the nature of modern politics. In the case of the United States, Gordon Wood's grand claim that the new nation witnessed in the early nineteenth century "a dispersion of authority and ultimately a diffusion of truth itself to a degree the world had never before seen," all despite the passing of the conservative federal Constitution, smacks of hyperbole.[32] Still, American historians, including Wood himself, have convincingly documented a marked decline in intellectual deference or taking claims to be truths on the authority of spokespersons alone (which may also help explain the concurrent rise of experts with their impersonal statistics). The trend started in the 1790s and accelerated into the new century, helped along considerably by the evangelicalism of the Second Great Awakening with its challenge to know for oneself. Some evidence comes from the directives of preachers and other public figures. Baptist Elias Smith, for example, told his lay audience in 1809 that all of them must be "wholly free to examine for ourselves what is truth, without being bound to a catechism, creed, confession of faith, discipline or any rule excepting the scriptures."[33] Other evidence, though, comes from ordinary people's challenges to the wisdom of the book-smart and to their ostensible stranglehold on the gentlemanly virtues of scrupulous honesty and knowledge. The early nineteenth century also bred a new kind of anti-intellectualism that turned on rejecting the elitism inherent in higher education as a whole (an attitude some might say was partly back in style now). As a letter writer to the *Raleigh Register* declared in 1829 in the Southern democratic spirit of the moment, "College learned persons give themselves great airs, are proud, and the fewer of them we have amongst us the better." As for universities as institutions, they were by definition "aristocratical" and opposed to "plain, simple, honest matter-of-fact republicanism."[34]

This unnamed correspondent in North Carolina actually sent off this message to the local press of Raleigh at an important juncture in the story of populist truth in North America. His missive appeared right on the heels of the 1828 presidential election, when Andrew Jackson became the first presidential candidate to capitalize on this new rhetoric, pitting himself as a self-described common man endowed with only his natural instincts and outsized persona (despite being one of the richest slave owners in Tennessee) against the multilingual, cosmopolitan, Harvard-educated, career politician and effete intellectual John Quincy Adams. Back at the turn of the century, Adams had tried to tarnish Jefferson as a savant and *philosophe*. However, this time, the tables were turned as a result of Jackson's new posture—and the fact that the American electorate had gotten considerably bigger. Jackson won decisively. "Harvard man" became a lasting slur.

Indeed, in Jackson's wake, elements of this familiar hortatory style and narrative mode worked their way seemingly permanently into the rhetoric of the two major American political parties, both of whom regularly insisted (and still do) that they embodied the will of the American people and a rebuke to special interests.[35] But in the United States, the populist approach to truth reached its fullest expression going forward in a series of sporadic challenges from third parties and protest movements, from the evocatively named nativist "Know Nothings" of the 1850s, to the renegade People's Party of 1890s (which gave us the term "populism" in the first place), to the Prohibitionists after the turn of the twentieth century, to the Alabama segregationist George Wallace in the 1960s.[36] Most of these challenges to the establishment and to the platforms of the core parties did not succeed in the long run or had very temporary moments of glory. But, arguably, they all played some role in shaping the big tent of the so-called post-truth populist epistemology of the present.

Only some of these insurrectionary movements were, like Prohibitionism, overtly religious in orientation. Others were thoroughly secular in their rhetoric and demands. Still, their common attachment to the idea of the people's instinctive knowledge created space for the acceptance of Christian faith and moral instinct as legitimate paths to truths that were useful in the political sphere—something that expert rule, which generally required the strict separation of interested private self from dispassionate public voice, or religious from secular orientation, did not.[37] Similarly, even though most of these political movements in the Jacksonian tradition offered a deeply masculinist conception of "the people" related to self-reliance and the ethos of producerism, with a lot of talk of "getting tough" on enemies, they also frequently encouraged women to join their ranks. In the process, they gave new credence as political assets to what were seen as feminine cognitive and ethical virtues—moral purity, intuition, and a homely command of kitchen-table logic—at a time when expertise, in its attachment to "universal" truth, remained primarily a male enterprise. Moreover, despite a generic hostility to plutocrats—or what were once called "speculators" and "monopolists"—American populist movements generally welcomed "honest" businesspeople, even very successful ones, and still do. What was valued here too was the businessperson's ostensibly practical, no-nonsense approach to the world. That is in marked contrast to the effect of, say, lawyers, whose elaborate procedures and arcane lingo led Alexis de Tocqueville to identify them already in the 1830s as the closest thing to an aristocratic element within American democratic culture.[38] It's also in contrast to people of color, male or female, since the populist ideal generally depended on an implicit or explicit appeal to whiteness. It is impossible to give exact epistemic or social parameters to what the People's Party platform called, in 1892, "the good sense of an intelligent people and the teachings of experience" on which the federal government should be refounded or to define the precise nature of that "old cab-drivin' logic" that Wallace would later juxtapose to the claims of "pseudo-theoreticians," "pseudo-social-engineers," and "Boston Harvard professors."[39] What's clear is that they belonged to a long tradition of claiming legitimacy, from the side of the overlooked, for everyday sources of truth, including some that might well be called dogmatic or absolutist, within the contours of a theoretically undogmatic liberalism.

Something similar has occurred in many other parts of the globe in the modern era. Both within existing democracies and in states where a subset of people (often, ironically, intellectuals) were or are looking to forge democracies, a populist conception of the people and their distinctive take on truth has waxed and waned. Histories of populism point to a grab bag of moments and milestones. There's the tradition of plebiscitary democracy associated with Louis-Napoleon in the France of the 1850s, which constituted an attempt to do away with all mediation or compromise with other forces and institutions in instituting the people's wishes (a pattern that would recur in modern French history). There's the Russian counterpart to the People's Party of the American South and Midwest: Narodnaya Volya, or the People's Will Party, founded in 1879 as an intellectual appeal to the virtuous peasantry to assume its rightful mantle as the true soul of the Russian nation. There's a wave of Latin America leaders—Juan and Eva Perón in Argentina, Getulio Vargas in Brazil, José María Velasco Ibarra in Ecuador, among others—who claimed in the 1930s and 1940s to embody the traditions and values of their respective nations in contradistinction to foreign-oriented elites. What's consistent, almost cliché, across these disparate movements is opposition to what traditional ruling elites have taken to be orthodox in terms of standard-bearers for truth claims and their institutions, procedures, and values. Consider this line from the celebrated Perón-era tango "Cambalache" (1935) lamenting this change in climate: "Everything is equal, nothing is better [now]; it's the same to be a jackass as a great professor."[40] That, and the elevation of a contrary way of thinking about knowledge and truth and what they will look like in the future. Perón's education minister Oscar Ivanissevich offered this fantasy of an alternative way forward in a

1948 speech: "We will teach first that children learn to live, afterward that they should learn to know. That they should know less and want more. That they should know less and think more. That they should know less and feel more. . . . We will not place in the fertile soil of their intelligence more seed than their natural capacity can nourish effectively. We will fight with all our might against parasitic . . . intellectualism."[41]

In other words, populists claim the coming reign of the people will be accompanied by a mental as much as, or rather than, economic revolution. Such ambitions seem to make almost predictable comebacks at times of perceived rapid change. But they also, now that democracy has become the default standard for politics in much of the world, seem to recur whenever old parties and other mediating institutions and their key personnel give the impression of having finally outlived their usefulness, including any real connection to ordinary people and their lives.

Our story takes a different turn, however, in the last decades of the twentieth century, especially in the north Atlantic. As the late 1970s turned into the 1980s in the United States, the angry outsider populism of George Wallace and the defensiveness of Richard Nixon, with its fixation on the bias of the "liberal media," came to an end. What replaced them was the sunnier, conservative mood of Ronald Reagan, the first president of the United States with a background in the entertainment industry. As the governor of California and then the leader of the nation, Reagan insisted that he was himself no expert on anything, not even politics. Rather, with his anecdotes and deceptively simple, folksy turns of phrase, he managed sometimes to sound like a latter-day Paine, while also suggesting that the kind of expertise (and specialized jargon) associated with lawyers, economists, and other social scientists was unnecessary for determining the principles of governance. "Common sense told us," he declared in his January 1989 Farewell Address to the Nation in an effort to explain his abiding economic philosophy, "that when you put a big tax on something, the people will produce less of it."[42] This mode proved particularly useful in mainstreaming positions that can, in fact, actually best be described as business-friendly and anti-regulatory—especially in contrast to both the People's Party of the 1890s and modern liberalism. In many ways, his greatest success came from attaching this distinctive rhetorical mode to the aim of undoing the New Deal state, adding the government to the list of the enemies of "the people."

Furthermore, on Reagan's watch, Nixon's talk of "middle America" and "the great silent majority" and "forgotten Americans" gave way to the Moral Majority as a critical political force. Simultaneously, in the 1980s, the American electorate came to include a large swathe of voters who, to a considerable degree, looked at the world from what they called a "Christian worldview," characterized by a literal reading of the Bible as settled truth. These same voters also increasingly distrusted the regulatory state (which had further expanded substantially in the 1970s, right along with religious conservatism) and its expert conclusions. At the urgings of evangelist political activists like David Barton and James Dobson, the force behind an educational initiative called the "Truth Project," religious conservatives came to reject academic historians' accounts of the past as suspect or even wrong, despite in many cases the preponderance of verifiable historical evidence, claiming they ran counter to the teachings of the Bible.[43] The same happened (with more immediately consequential results) in the realm of the physical and natural sciences, especially when it came to questions where science and government policy intersected, as around such pressing issues as AIDS, stem-cell research, and climate change.[44] The evidence-based and tested findings of doctors and academic researchers, and not just the policy proposals that resulted, found themselves increasingly under attack, from the halls of Congress to a whole new world of alternative media outlets, including direct mail, radio talk shows, cable news, and textbooks pushing alternative interpretations, often from the perspective of common sense combined with the absolute "truth" of biblical revelation.

This epistemic breach seems to have grown even wider as of late. A subculture now exists of people on the far left who are convinced that the government has become beholden to industry rather than liberal ideology and that they are being systematically lied to (by the National Institutes of Health or the Food and Drug Administration or the *New York Times* or some combination of the above) about phenomena ranging from vaccines and genetically modified foods to chemtrails.[45] However, this phenomenon has become considerably more pronounced on the right. Studies show that between the mid-1970s and 2010, public confidence in findings associated with the scientific establishment declined substantially and steadily among one, but only one, major sector of the American population: self-described political conservatives, many of whom also identify as religious conservatives.[46] Moreover, conservative skepticism now extends to ostensibly nonpartisan, social science–based research institutions, from the FBI to the Congressional Budget Office, as well as to universities, research laboratories, and the majority of the press, all understood as strongholds of the liberal elite. Where once the mainstream right was reliably drawn to establishment beachheads, and radicals on the left were those with epistemological qualms regarding official truth, that is no longer primarily the case. Trust in institutions dedicated to knowledge production and dissemination (as opposed to, say, policing) has become characteristic of the American center and left alone. Directly in relation to the growth of the expert-led state, populism has more and more been remade and redeployed as a moral and epistemic framework for the defense of small and, even, say some critics, "post-policy" government in which officials, elected or not, try not to do much at all outside of the defense of national borders.[47]

In Europe, the story has played out differently. By the early 1990s, post-Reagan, post–Margaret Thatcher, and post–Berlin Wall, mainstream continental European politicians also began to look for benefits to be derived from taking a populist rhetorical stance against expertise in politics, including in the scientific realm. Consider the highly establishment, conservative Jacques Chirac running for election to the French presidency in France in 1995 and attacking the "technostructure" and "experts" who had confiscated power from the people, giving priority to "statistics" over the "popular will" and thereby disengaging from "reality."[48] Such statements hit all the standard notes, despite Chirac's own very technocratic background in that most technocratic of states, France. But the real story in Europe at the end of the twentieth century was the rise to prominence of alternative, nonmainstream parties that, in the context of parliamentary democracies where they might have real influence, made anti-institutionalism and power to "the people," often in a nationalist vein, a centerpiece of their appeal.

Some of these parties, like the socialist-populist PASOK party in Greece, situated themselves on the edges of the left. But those that really flourished in Europe in new ways starting in the 1990s were primarily on the right and far right. That's when, for example, his fortunes rising, the Holocaust-denying Jean-Marie Le Pen of France embraced as watchwords both the people's "good sense" and the actual term "populism," and similarly, Austria's Jörg Haider issued declarations like "average citizens often have a better sense of things than these top men in politics who think that they need to explain to the people what moves them."[49] Rightist leaders also identified as the chief villain something of a sitting duck: the European Union's complex, difficult-to-fathom organization and decision-making processes, the transnational equivalent of Washington's bureaucracy and "inside-the-beltway" mentality, especially after the Maastricht Treaty of 1992, which authorized the future creation of the euro and Eurozone, revealed the depth of division on the Europe question everywhere. Le Pen *père* and his Front National insisted that global capitalists and statist technocrats were working hand in hand with little interest in the fortunes of the French population or their cost. Nigel Farage and the UK Independence Party (UKIP) promised instead to represent those whom Brussels and London had left behind. Both parties also attacked the growing presence of foreigners on their national turf. Nationalist, anti-immigrant, and antitechnocratic themes thus merged in a bid to expand rightist parties' support. Challenges to the bailouts of Greece, Ireland, Spain, and Portugal after the economic crisis of 2009, combined with hardline approaches to the ongoing refugee crisis, have only added to their success in very recent years, with the Brexit decision of 2016 (and the lies that sold it, including its potential benefits to British healthcare) as possibly exhibit A.[50] Asked to name economists who back the United Kingdom's exit from the European Union, Michael Gove, a leading Tory Brexit proponent, said, "I think people in this country have had enough of experts." To which Labor Brexit advocate Gisela Stuart later added, "There is only one expert that matters and that's you, the voter."[51]

But Euroscepticism and the peculiarities of European politics alone cannot explain this recent strain of populism, especially since the United States seems now to be catching up with it. A host of long-term, global trends has also shaped what appears to be a transnational political turn since the 1980s, and they need to be considered too in light of their impact on changing conceptions of truth in the democratic public sphere. First, politics, not to mention knowledge about it, has gotten ever more complex in recent decades, from the issues at stake, to the procedures it follows, to the language it employs to explain itself. Problems, as well as bureaucracies for approaching them, are now also largely multinational in scope—think refugees, nuclear weapons, terrorism, trade, or, for that matter, fishing rights—and thus often beyond the capacity of any national state, not to mention private citizens or citizen groups, to tackle or even fully comprehend. A new kind of de facto opacity has set in even as we drown in information.

At the same time, the growth of multicultural societies has also unseated any stable or fixed way of seeing the world (if such a thing ever existed), instead pushing pluralism and relativism well beyond the boundaries imagined in the eighteenth century, when religious minorities, people of color, women, foreigners, and native peoples were all formally excluded from most meaningful debate. From India to the United States, the flourishing of a plethora of different voices in the public sphere, an effect of the displacements created by the aftermath of colonialism, extended warfare, and global capitalism, has proved both intellectually exhilarating and destabilizing. In this context, identities attached to different stances on knowledge (being for or against "science" as a form of authority that can justify other claims, for example) have proliferated right along with ethnic identities and other forms of tribalism.

Perhaps most significantly, no real response has emerged, especially in the United States, but also in democracies in Latin America, South Asia, and Europe, to the problems of advanced capitalism, where inequality in income (which tends then to extend to everything else, from healthcare to schooling) continues to expand, and even politics seems to have been captured by moneyed interests in newly extreme ways just as Keynesianism at the state level has been declining. Expertise, even objectivity, can seem inseparable from neo-liberalism, meaning most often economist-driven, market-based solutions.[52] In this context, is it any wonder that trust has deteriorated, even in previously esteemed institutions? Or that popular desire has grown for the very opposite: throwing out all kinds of intermediaries, along with the complex language and processes associated with them, and finding simple, emotionally satisfying responses as replacements?

As a result, the taste for the blandest forms of populism has become so ubiquitous that we have hardly even noticed its prevalence, at least in American political rhetoric, in the early twenty-first century. Both Presidents George W. Bush and Barack Obama, one the (Republican) Ivy-educated scion of an oligarchic family with roots in Connecticut and Texas and the other a (Democratic) Ivy-educated multiracial professor of law raised in Hawaii, insisted at times on adopting a folksy tone, itself borrowed from distinguished predecessors ranging from Jackson to Franklin Delano Roosevelt, and on declaring their enduring commitment to common sense. They did so whenever they wanted to convey that they were regular guys, despite their actual class backgrounds, relying on the same kind of everyday logic that ordinary people do as they go about their ordinary business, far from the corridors of power. They also did so when they were eager to signal that consensus existed even when it did not. Evoking common sense, as opposed to statistics or philosophical principles, has become a conventional way for politicians to indicate that they aim to transcend partisan politics and simply implement the solution we'd all agree upon if we got rid of the bickering, overeducated experts and their beholden, ideologically driven colleagues. Think "commonsense gun laws" or "commonsense immigration reform" or the Common Sense Health Care Reform and Affordability Act of 2009.[53] They sound too obvious to think about twice (though they've also all failed to become legislation), and that's just the point.

Of course, all that talk doesn't mean either president or his aides eschewed expertise when needed. Obama certainly didn't. On the contrary, he seemed to many Americans the very embodiment of elite modes of deliberation and knowledge production. And even George W. Bush, who famously *did* dismiss the findings of much of the intelligence community when it came to Iraq and weapons of mass destruction and with disastrous results, mixed the technocratic and commonsensical together as needed. So have, in recent years, the French president Nicolas Sarkozy and the Italian prime minister (and not incidentally, media tycoon) Silvio Berlusconi, who frequently both said they spoke for the people while actually taking a managerial approach to politics. The political scientist Pierre Musso has even given this style a clever name: "Sarkoberlusconisme."[54]

From this one vantage point, then, it is hard not to see a certain amount of continuity in the Trump moment. The current U.S. president began his quixotic campaign in 2016 as the embodiment of a recognizable kind of right-wing, but still essentially democratic, populist style. Instead of deference to well-trained scientists, academics, journalists, and even governmental authorities, he (though actually also Ivy-educated and a self-professed billionaire) touted the true wisdom of "the people" and the "silent majority" as opposed to "special interests."[55] In place of fancy studies built on research, data, and modeling, he promised reports on the state of our world derived from ordinary sense experience and instinct cultivated in the real world of buying and selling, not more intellectual or rarified spaces. As Trump told a journalist at the *Washington Post* before he won the presidency, he does not need to read or study history because he has always made decisions "with very little knowledge other than the knowledge I had, plus the words 'common sense,' because I have a lot of common sense and I have a lot of business ability"—an idea he's repeated as president in explaining why he doesn't need to prepare for summits and meetings and can rely on "just my touch, my feel."[56] He also made much from the beginning of being beholden to no persons or institutions, rich beyond most Americans' imaginings, but regular in his tastes and convictions.

Certainly, his brand of populism was nastier, crasser, and more belligerent than most of what had come down the pike in mainstream Republican circles previously. His blistering attacks on the press and political opponents made him sound a lot more like a latter-day George Wallace than Ronald Reagan. Witness his savaging of "Crooked Hillary" [Clinton], whom he painted (hyperbolically and nastily and not totally inaccurately) as standing for all the sins of the professional expert wrapped into one: venality, internationalism, physical weakness, an inclination toward social engineering in favor of women and minorities, and a grand passion for pulling the wool over the rest of the people's eyes. But in terms of instincts, he never strayed that far from "Sarkoberlusconisme," Reagan's homilies, or, even more, the erstwhile pizza-mogul-turned-politician Herman Cain, who ran for the Republican nomination for president in 2012 calling himself the president of the University of Common Sense and claiming to have a father with a PhD in the subject. The campaign, in many respects, despite Trump's longstanding taste for lies and exaggerations, fell squarely in the old tradition of the outsider coming in to bring a healthy dose of people-based truth to the byzantine ways of Washington.

From the beginning, many of Trump's policy proposals followed in this populist epistemic vein too. When
he announced a few months into his campaign that the
answer to illegal immigration was building a very big wall
along the southern border of the United States, it was clear
that—the racism of the idea aside—he was speaking in a
familiar do-as-I-do-in-my-own-backyard mode. If you
keep your neighbors out of your yard with a fence, your
nation should do the same, just make it bigger.[57] Ditto
for problems of trade and finance. Out of money? Don't
spend so much. Repeatedly, he insisted that solving America's problems was, for someone with his street smarts
and real-world experience, going to be nothing less than
"easy" (though he's had to backtrack some on that particular claim). No info or data was required, and it might
even get in the way. By now, it is a familiar pattern on the
right and, some might argue, on the fringes of the left too.
Trump could be said simply to represent the apotheosis
of this longstanding anti-intellectual, antiprofessional current that Hofstadter long ago identified (with dismay) as a
peculiarly American trait but that actually seems today to
have fairly global reach.

Still, conventional or not, the apotheosis of populist truth
within democracy, including in the Trumpian vein, poses
some serious risks for the future—just as a democracy
veering toward epistocracy does. Also, we have had strong
hints as of late that something new *is* afoot and that we
should think about rupture in this story as well as continuity. Let's start with the risks, moving from least to greatest,
and then finally turn to the question of how to situate the
current moment within history.

One major risk is simply that populist leaders and their parties end up, like technocrats, crafting very bad policies, policies that do nothing to address the real problems of real people and even run the risk of exacerbating them. When, for example, experts of all kinds warn that plans to build a wall at the U.S.-Mexican border ignore the facts—and not just structural or economic ones like how difficult and costly it would be to put a wall through a river, but also data about who is crossing the border now and how and why—there is a good chance that forging ahead anyway is a bad idea. At best, it will result in waste and folly in the service of a politics of pure symbolism. At worst, it will produce unnecessary human tragedies. But if the judgments of the best informed among us cannot be trusted as sources of knowledge, and voters and their representatives must rely almost entirely on their own necessarily limited experience in the world or emotional reactions to the situation, then solutions built on dangerous oversimplifications and false analogies (from the kitchen table to the nation, from the backyard to international borders) are bound to result, regardless of anyone's good or bad intentions.

Then there's the possibility, again whether deliberate or inadvertent, of a politics too dependent on a populist conception of truth creating lasting and dangerous schisms in the social fabric. Listening only to the sense of the "real" people or in-group, while sidelining experts and opponents and other outliers as purveyors of nonsense, not only keeps important dissenting voices out of conversations based on point of view, thereby curtailing the real debate on which democracy should thrive. It also runs the risk of producing scapegoats of the kind that fuel nativism, racism, and anti-Semitism and the curtailment of civil liberties, especially if these outsiders are described as enemies and traitors and not just people with whom one disagrees. Ultimately, a strident populism increases the possibility of real violence between tribes too. This is, in short, precisely the potential tyranny of the majority that so worried the authors of the U.S. Constitution back in the 1780s and that they tried so hard to think of formal ways to prevent.

For most alarmingly of all, with populist truth we ultimately run into a threat to the survival of democracy itself. As we've seen, the democratic imaginary has depended since the eighteenth century on a vision of active debate but also cooperation across wealth, educational, religious, and ideological divides, fueled by a commitment to plain speech, free speech, and a variety of mediating and educational institutions, starting with the press and now including public schools, political parties, research institutes, and more. Yet this system for arriving at truths has always been minimalist in spirit and fraught in practice even at the level of the most basic forms of information and their interpretation. And when trust in knowledge-producing institutions declines too much, and everything, from the evening news to the president's word, starts to seem equally a matter of opinion as opposed to hardnosed, indisputable fact no matter its source, then it becomes impossible to imagine ever arriving at even the loose general consensus, the "serviceable truths" or "public knowledge" necessary for modestly effective conversation across the aisle or other boundaries.

That could mean that deadlock, dysfunction, or even some form of anarchy becomes the new normal in political life. However, it also opens the door, at least in principle, for one charismatic leader or leaders, preying on popular resentment and fear as well as popular suscep- tibility to flattery, to claim to be able to know the will of the people and to channel their commonsense view of the world better than the people themselves. The framers of the American Constitution called such people not dem- ocrats or republicans but demagogues. Because in such conditions, it was imagined, a leader or two could, in the name of a compliant people, gradually dismantle the last remnants of pluralism and liberalism that self-rule com- bined with undogmatic truth require, consolidate his or her own power, and openly engage in lies and corruption of the kind populists generally start out railing against, all without much pushback from a dormant or nonfunc- tional civil society. We've actually seen something like this happen before. Democratically elected Fascist leaders between the two world wars provide case studies. So do Viktor Orbán in Hungary and Recep Tayyip Erdoğan in Turkey, with their taste for dismantling institutions and jailing unwelcome "truth-sayers," be they professors, polit- ical opponents, or media critics, in just the last few years. We have not, to date, seen such a development as part of the post-1776 American political tradition.

Which brings us back to Trump and his administra- tion, spokespeople, and mass of ordinary supporters. Is it possible that, as president rather than candidate, Trump also represents an impending break or at least substan- tial twist in the larger story of post-Enlightenment and even post-Reagan commonsense populism? The answer is certainly yes. This is not because he has moved back toward technocracy, despite his administration's anti- regulatory, libertarian bent on certain issues, such as the environment. And it's not because he has simply turned up the volume on an old discourse. Rather, it's because he appears determined to engage (to the degree he can get away with it) in the kind of undemocratic demagoguery, or "authoritarian posturing," as one journalist recently put it, with which democratic populism always flirts at its edges.[58] Not only does the president (like his fan base) show a predilection for mob violence combined with race-baiting and pomp and circumstance; display constant contempt for the separation of powers, the free press, and other institutions for protecting dissent; shower praise on strongmen around the world, from Kim Jong Un of North Korea to Russia's Vladimir Putin; and claim he, Donald Trump, can "do it alone"—all classic quasi-authoritarian poses. Most stunningly, the president of the United States has repeatedly—to the astonishment of many observers—denied the validity of any empirically demonstrable and shared reality altogether.

On almost his first day in office, Trump looked at photos of his own inauguration, declared the crowd the biggest ever, and made everyone around him repeat this, though we could all *see* that this was blatantly untrue. This, to come back to where we started, is a kind of compulsive lying that isn't designed to fool as much as to display power: over everyone and everything. Sometimes the president declares that the exterior world is incomprehensible, mere chaos that defies understanding ("What the hell is going on?" is a favorite phrase). But other times, he simply insists the world is the way he says it is, regardless of all evidence to the contrary. In effect, Trump often encourages the public *not* to believe its eyes, to ignore commonsense perceptions right along with expertise. As he exhorted a room full of members of the Veterans of Foreign Wars in Kansas City in a moment of defiance in July 2018, "Stick with us. Don't believe the crap you see from these people, the fake news. . . . What you're seeing and what you're reading is not what's happening." The *New York Times*'s reporters who described the speech called his goal "bending the truth to his own narrative."[59] We might put it differently and say he's rejecting not just the undogmatic Enlightenment approach to truth upon which democracies still, more than two centuries later, depend as an ideal, but also the existence of any truth at all apart from what he can get away with calling by that name in the political arena. In this context, truth, or the representation of reality, becomes nothing more than a matter of political might. That's why Trump prefers outlets like mass rallies or Twitter (today's version of Perón's radio) that allow him to convey his messages directly to his supporters, without any intermediaries or fact-checkers getting in the way. That's also why he is always insisting that election results are numerically flawed unless they show him as the winner. In the end, the Trump era builds on but also marks a real departure from the traditional populist position in which blunt honesty and common sense are supposed to rule the day.

Again, it is Arendt who explains why this matters. From *The Origins of Totalitarianism*, published in 1951, to her late 1960s and early 1970s musings on truth and falsehood in democratic politics, Arendt repeatedly called attention to a very particular kind of lying that she associated with the authoritarian governments of mid-twentieth-century Europe. This was a form of dissembling that was so brazen and comprehensive, so far from standard political fibbing and selective spin, that it left a population essentially impotent. People living in totalitarian environments, she proposed, typically saw no choice but to acquiesce in the illogic of it all, ignoring the erasure of any distinctions between fact and fiction and considering anything possible. Or they cynically disengaged, trusting no one and nothing. For "the result of a consistent and total substitution of lies for factual truth," or what we sometimes now call gaslighting on a massive scale, was inevitably nothing less than the demise, individually and collectively, of "the sense by which we take our bearings in the real world."[60] The only other remaining option in such circumstances— and the one that was most difficult to pull off and took the most courage, Arendt pointed out—was to work to make commonsense truth-telling into a weapon in the business of resistance, in effect, to turn what I'm calling a populist epistemology on its head and use it politically to try to restore some kind of normalcy. In such circumstances, "living in truth," to use Václav Havel's famous expression of the 1970s, became a political act.[61] So far, that has not happened in any widespread way among American Republican voters.

It is, however, also not clear if Trump will succeed in creating the kind of world that Arendt writes about in *The Origins of Totalitarianism*—or even that he really aims to do so. The next chapter will consider what's different about the very recent past, but also all that might keep us from going off the rails. What's clear as I write is only that the American population, like that of post-Brexit Britain, and indeed Erdogan's Turkey and Orbán's Hungary, is internally divided.[62] In the United States, Trump has been met with a furious reaction by some very large number of partially stunned citizens who are trying to reassert democratic norms via rallies in the streets and the institutional pressure of courts and newspapers. Many others have received him with an open embrace. Some of the latter don't mind that he is lying because they see a deeper truth than a surface one in his description of a declining America and the fears he stokes about immigrants, protesters, and nefarious reporters. Some are perhaps just eager to see the kind of consternation the president's antics cause among otherwise cocky, know-it-all liberals—which is probably not a sufficient ground for imagining a shift in truth perception in the culture at large. Also, populism is often more successful as a logic or narrative for opposition than it is as a style of governance. Once it is assimilated into a ruling creed, it frequently turns into nothing more than a rhetorical cover (albeit with more talk of crises and enemies) for the same stances and policies being pushed by everyone else.

Several new ironies thus become apparent at this chapter's close. One is that populists often think they are shoring up democratic truth-telling, or finally bringing it to fruition, when they are, just as often, unwittingly undermining it. Another is that though they are provoked in good part by hatred for technocracy and the social groups and institutions of which it is constituted, populists end up fighting many of the same battles using many of the same weapons as technocrats. In the end, dyed-in-the-wool populists and technocrats mimic one another in rejecting mediating bodies (including often the major political parties since the late nineteenth century), procedural legitimacy, and the very idea that fierce competition among ideas is necessary for arriving at political truth. In many ways, the key risk of our post-truth era is not that facts really will disappear and never be heard from again, despite much recent hand-wringing on the subject. It is that the particular, old-fashioned mythology around truth, which remains central to the modern liberal democratic imaginary, will turn out to have outlived its relevancy and its appeal, and we will have nothing to put in its place.[63]

Democracy in an Age of Lies

It's one of the oldest dreams around. One day, a single language, a single grammar, a single learning method, or even a single repository like a world library will lead to universal knowledge. Universal knowledge will, in turn, produce harmony among all peoples and maybe even lasting world peace. You can find versions of this myth throughout history, from Ptolemy's efforts in manuscript collecting in Alexandria in the third century BCE to the introduction of Esperanto as a lingua franca at the end of the nineteenth century CE.[1]

Such an idea might well have become obsolete by our own era. Knowledge, after all, has steadily proliferated and diversified over all those years. Arguably, there is just too much "truth" out there by now. Instead, the opposite happened at the end of the twentieth and the start of the twenty-first centuries: this ancient dream came to seem newly within reach, a potential byproduct of the great technological and cultural changes of our times. It also quickly took on a demophilic cast, as fits the attachment to democratic governance characteristic of the era after World

War II and, especially, the post-1989 era. As recently as a few years ago, evangelists of the Internet were still holding out the promise that, by dint of its vast reach as well as low cost to consumers, we, the citizens of the twenty-first century, were fast approaching the point at which the entirety of knowledge would be democratized, equally available to everyone everywhere. Then liberal democracy itself, as the dominant and preferred system for organizing the human world, would naturally follow, capitalism in tow.

At home, we'd be liberated from an old formula in which economic inequality naturally reinforced information asymmetry, and vice versa, even as we continued to think of ideas existing in a marketplace, freely competing for our approval. Outdated hierarchies of epistemic authority, whether political, economic, or cultural, would likely evaporate too. For once we were all able to get our news directly from the source or sources, we would no longer need to treat television network news anchors, or any other cultural figureheads, as modern oracles. And maybe most significantly, in still nondemocratic polities, like postrevolutionary Cuba, the Internet would break down the state's media monopoly and produce a true public sphere in which citizens would finally be able to locate one another, claim their rights, and engage in new forms of social and political action designed to secure them. All over the globe, in other words, the Internet would favor the oppressed over the oppressor. Its power as a source of emancipation would prove unbeatable.[2]

No one is so sanguine these days. Just as earlier communicative breakthroughs—the printing press, radio, television—spawned new forms of techno-utopianism, they also all generated second thoughts, and sometimes real panic, about the dangers that had been unleashed along with the promise. One need not be a Luddite or total stick-in-the-mud to see that the fearmongers were often right. The advent of mechanical printing in the late fifteenth century, for example, proved an almost immediate boon to scholarship and the international circulation of ideas. But then it also helped produce the deep cultural fractures and violence of the Reformation just a few decades later—and in ways that permanently reshaped Christian Europe.[3] The problem is that technologies do not arise in *terra vida*. Rather, they always intersect with other social, political, economic, even intellectual currents, potentially fueling new moral and epistemic crises around truth rather than resolving them. If the big story in the 1990s centered on the glowing and twinned futures of democracy and knowledge as the technological fulfillment of an Enlightenment dream, that vision seems now to be crashing back to earth, with the rest of us left wondering: What went so wrong—and why now? How did we end up not in the age of total knowledge but in a new age of lies?

The answer certainly doesn't depend on any one figure. To return to the main example of the moment, few commentators think Donald Trump is fully responsible even for the phenomenon of Donald Trump, and almost all take him to be but a player, albeit a powerful one, in a much larger development that, as we've seen, frequently gets labeled "post-truth."[4] The same goes even for leaders of nations much more successfully authoritarian than the United States today. But then it's also not quite right to see the present moment as somehow entirely preordained, set in motion by the interrelated but hostile trajectories of democracy and bureaucracy as explained by Weber, or to look only to long-term patterns pitting experts and elites against populists, cosmopolitans versus patriots. For something *has* happened to bring this old conflict to a head, something that, to keep our primary example going, makes America under Trump feel more like a caesura in the history of modern democracy than just an acceleration of preexisting trends.

To take stock of this change, we need to turn an eye too, in this short history, to the short-term causes that, rightly or wrongly, have drawn the majority of press commentary, especially in liberal and centrist establishment circles, as of late. These are, primarily, developments in philosophy, entertainment, technology, and indeed media, innovations often a bit to the side of political history even as they have become implicated in it. The idea is to assess the ways that these recent cultural shifts have contributed not only to the recent rise of popular truth-challenged leaders in many parts of the world, including the United States, but, more fundamentally, to the undermining of the foundational yet always precarious democratic take on truth that has been an operative ideal since the eighteenth century.

The first such factor that many commentators have pointed to goes by the shorthand label postmodernism. You have undoubtedly been reading about it in connection to politics all over the place in the last year or two. The standard argument is that, in the realm of ideas, what began in Berkeley, New York, Paris, Ljubljana, and other intellectual centers as a highbrow, left-wing effort to cast suspicion upon experts and their claims to truth has recently come back, several decades later, to bite the left on the nose. So when we hear Trump spokesperson and former New York mayor Rudolph Giuliani defending the

American president by saying "truth isn't truth," or Kelly-anne Conway, another Trump mouthpiece, talking of "alternative facts," we are simply witnessing late-twentieth-century postmodernist epistemology in its new, weaponized right-wing mode.[5]

The story usually begins in the late 1960s, when transatlantic leftists denounced "objective" journalism as a prop for power, if not a set of outright strategic lies, under the cloud of the Algerian War and then the war in Vietnam. It then continues with a chronicle of a deeper, more profound assault on universal or definitive knowledge taking hold, especially in the American university world. From the 1960s social constructivism of Thomas Kuhn's *The Structure of the Scientific Revolution* and Peter Berger and Thomas Luckmann's *The Social Construction of Reality,* to the feminist scholarship of the 1970s that emphasized epistemic difference, to the taste for French poststructuralist theory and deconstruction that suffused the more chic precincts of American academia in the 1980s, the humanities and even some of the social sciences absorbed and disseminated the idea that most claims to capital-T truth were hogwash. That's because humans to a considerable extent construct the reality that they see around them—and do so in different ways in different cultures and moments and according to their varied social positions and relations to power. What's more, humans can never really escape the constructs that they create, starting with language, to view the world any differently. All of us are constrained by larger structural forces to perceive and to think the particular way we do. Or so the argument goes.

And from this perspective, artists, writers, dramatists, and filmmakers all over the globe, under the banner of both postmodernist epistemology and identity politics, have been reinforcing this skeptical and relativist disposition for several decades now. How? First, by producing work that further undermines any remaining consoling notion we might want to harbor about the possibility of finding an omnipotent, disinterested point of view from which to see the world around us, and second, by celebrating personal and partial truth in its stead. The consequence, claim jubilantly told-you-so realist philosophers like Daniel Dennett, is that Foucault-loving intellectuals and literary types ended up handing the right wing everywhere a gift: an intellectually dubious but rhetorically effective way of talking about truth that could ultimately be turned against the left to justify a raw power grab. All of which ostensibly explains why Roger Stone and Jacques Derrida have recently been showing up in articles together. This is a story about philosophy run amuck, topped with a dollop of karmic justice.[6]

But does this narrative have any merit as a claim about the impact of ideas on history as opposed to an antipostmodernist polemic? Is it all bunk? It is possible, after all, to find some structural similarities between camps, starting with the fact that postmodernists and the current post-truth right (like Fascists before them) share a generic enemy in Enlightenment rationalism and the authority of something called "science." Also, the flourishing of identity politics, in both its progressive, left-leaning and newer, white-nationalist varieties, suggests that at least some platitudes associated with the radical edge of late twentieth-century thought have trickled down into the political culture at large, including the idea of challenging structural forms of marginalization. As for the "liberalocracy":

one reason it is so fixated on questions of truth in public life right now, and questions of truth suddenly seem so centrally *political,* might well stem from the fact that its members have done a lot of thinking about its meaning in recent years. (This book, for example, would not be possible without a whole lot of preceding scholarly literature, much of it cited in my notes, that has encouraged historians, not to mention writers and artists, to think long and hard since the 1980s about questions like who determines truth, by what criteria do they do so, and how have those conceptions changed over time.)

However, this argument for the impact of postmodern thought on the truth-starved political culture of today largely fails, *pace* the pundits, for two reasons. First, it is typically based on a misreading of the nature of postmodernist claims, which are actually quite consonant with democratic antidogmatism. Second, it depends upon a misunderstanding of causation.

In terms of philosophy, to attribute to Foucault or Richard Rorty or, really, most of postmodernism's main exponents the rejection of *anything* constituting truth, starting with facts, is to distort their claims. As legal theorist Frederick Schauer neatly explains, it was and remains entirely possible to believe that much of the world we experience is socially constructed without denying the existence of mind-independent facts and thus of a mind-independent reality behind them—or, in his examples, that money, law, and the Republican Party are social artifacts, but that zebras and gravity have an existence apart from human creation and comprehension, and, we might add, that the Republican Party was founded in 1854, which was twenty-six years after the creation of the Democratic

Party.[7] Few so-called postmodernists would likely disagree despite some occasional silly statements to the contrary (which inevitably provide fuel for cooked-up conservative media scandals). For the postmodern message—if we can generalize—has largely been not that facts cannot exist or that they cannot be falsified or verified, but rather that how they are chosen, expressed, valued, and deployed is always a question of power relations, and there is no single, correct, "objective" way to interpret them. Furthermore, none of what postmodern thinkers have to say indicates the wholesale rejection of truth on ethical grounds—the idea that truth doesn't matter or shouldn't have any more hold over us than belief or desire—that is often attributed to our post-truth moment. Post-truth and postmodernism are, in the main, false cognates, as are their progenitors.

The same holds true for artists. The discovery of the incommensurability of various points of view or the untrustworthy narrator is hardly a recent phenomenon. Writers and painters have always taken mimesis, or the question of how to represent reality, to be their bread and butter. And since well before the era of Nietzsche and Freud, artists of all kinds have also reminded us of our perceptual limitations—say, that retinal vision is superficial and distorting or that realism as a style constitutes its own form of deception—and proposed abstraction, montage, or some other seemingly "unnatural" technique as ultimately a more accurate way to convey the truth of the interior or even exterior world. In the process, they have also challenged us to reconsider which kinds of truths we can access and what eludes us, that is, to think constructively about what we take to be real. When the Russian avant-garde filmmaker Dziga Vertov, in his 1928 essay "Factory of Facts," spoke of the limitations of "life as it is, seen by the imperfect human eye," his goal was not to manipulate others into taking untruth for reality in the Trumpist fashion. Rather it was to suggest that the camera or "aided eye," in the hands of the artist, offered new means to higher, transformative truths appropriate for a revolutionary cultural movement aimed at shattering the status quo.[8] That's essentially what avant-gardes have been proposing from the nineteenth century to today. Postmodernism has little monopoly here.

But even if we stick more modestly to identifying a loose set of shared concerns across postmodernist and post-truth terrains, this claim about intellectual filiation still largely fails. In yet another irony, the separation of the academy, not to mention the world of progressive art, from daily life—a phenomenon that developed right alongside the specialization and professionalization of intellectual labor in the modern era—has in recent years made the impact on a broad public of *any* important philosophical or aesthetic currents minimal, to say the least. Rorty, with his provocative claims like "truth is what your contemporaries let you get away with," might occasionally sound like a precursor to Trump.[9] But context matters to meaning. When Trump, an expert in the domain of marketing, says something similar, he's echoing a long history of huckster salesmen and would-be strongmen, not postmodern ironists like Rorty. Similarly, there is little evidence that the populist voter attracted to a commonsense politics or even a post-truth one has been shaped by French techniques of literary deconstruction or by the experimental novel or even by Hollywood's efforts at bringing complex, multiviewpoint storytelling to the screen. That's especially true since we have become more balkanized as cultural consumers as well. On the contrary, despite a few quips from former Trump strategist Steve Bannon about "deconstructing" the administrative state, the populist right has spent much more energy denouncing the academy as a site of leftist indoctrination dependent upon the propagation of a dangerous moral and cognitive relativism than it ever has on embracing the now slightly dated perspective of an older generation of comparative literature scholars.[10] If anything, the main political effect of postmodernism, as Rorty himself lamented toward the end of his career, was to draw the energy of the intellectual left away from significant engagement in "real" politics associated with socioeconomic reform and social justice and to replace hope with knowingness and resignation.[11]

More important, certainly, in making the rejection of verified truth one of the signature political values of the current moment has been a shift in the world of mass entertainment and, indeed, mass media. This story begins, in the North American context, not with translations of Derrida or Foucault but with the explosion of political talk radio in the 1990s. The ball got firmly rolling with the repeal, in 1987, of the Federal Communications Commission's Fairness Doctrine, which had mandated since 1949 that radio audiences be provided with news in a fashion that was "honest, equitable, and balanced," meaning committed to truth-telling and representative of a variety of viewpoints. Partisan talk radio took off in the aftermath. That was especially the case on the political right, where—released from this restriction—reporting, entertainment, and opinionated ranting merged in a popular new format.[12] Rush Limbaugh's show, the gold standard, became national in 1988.

Shortly thereafter, a novel kind of cable television news, it too a product of the deregulation of information, entered the American public sphere. In 1996, Fox News, the pioneer in the genre, gave up the establishment television news model associated with the major networks and public broadcasting and turned a mixture of current events and partisan political opinion into a twenty-four-hour-a-day enterprise.[13] Again, the new format worked more successfully on the political right, where it could be touted as an alternative to a biased mainstream. (With a wink at its audience, Fox News originally adopted the tagline "Fair and Balanced." Executives very recently added "Real News. Real Honest Opinion." In all cases, the idea was not to suggest actual impartiality but rather a counterweight to the allegedly skewed "fake news" of the liberal establishment.) And to keep audiences listening and watching—and thus advertisers happy—for hour after hour, the leading cable TV hosts, like their radio counterparts, worked hard at riling up their fans. The key was found to lie in constantly recycling tales of outrage at the events of the day, employing attack-dog talking heads to amplify these points often in mock-debate format, and relentlessly selling a one-sided, often vitriolic political storyline along with various consumer products.

These new media spaces soon resembled echo chambers or virtual gated neighborhoods. Within their confines, far-fetched ideas that had largely been kept at bay by polite society could get bandied about without serious challenges (indeed, they were often relabeled, as in the case of hosts like Glenn Beck or Bill O'Reilly, as common sense).

Fears—of the power of immigrants, the "deep state," the media itself—could also be stoked through constant repetition. The opposition, meanwhile, turned increasingly into an object of righteous hatred rather than simply the locus of differing views. Audiences for political entertainment became more and more like the angry and proudly partisan callers to sports-fan radio shows, just ones who'd substituted their political party for their favorite team. Some portion of viewers also began to embrace a certain amount of lying, seeing defeat of the enemy as more important than getting it all right (a Machiavellian possibility that Arendt never accounted for in her catalogue of the political functions of various kinds of modern lies).

At the same time, though, successful opinion programs like *The O'Reilly Factor* on Fox also made "experts" seem like people who simply liked yelling a lot, and who had unshakably partisan takes on the world, since facts could so easily be instrumentalized or even made up for political gain, entertainment value or both. "Reality TV" and late-night political-humor shows, which became more likely to skew explicitly left starting with Comedy Central's *Daily Show* in the Jon Stewart years, made sure to hammer that point too, exposing all the dumb stuff that pundits said while confusing truth and fiction, celebrity and authority even further.[14] By the early 2000s, these developments in "infotainment," alongside the decline of traditional news forms, had begun to transform American political culture. The far right side of the Republican Party, in particular, figured out how to benefit (Trump could be called a direct product of this media machine and, now, an amplification system for it, since cable television is also where he gets his own information). Already in the George W. Bush years, the deck was being stacked against efforts to maintain any widely shared standards of epistemic authority, thereby stoking conflict between adherents of different understandings of truth. The delegitimization of the "mainstream media" and the flourishing of privately produced TV propaganda—a fancy word for *real* fake news—generated some substantial differences between the American and European political landscapes in the first years of the twenty-first century.

Then along came the technological breakthrough that is the Internet and, especially, powerful social media companies like Facebook, YouTube, and Twitter that set up shop, circa 2005, within its terrain.[15] Thanks to social media, adaptations of these new political cultural norms associated with American call-in radio and other forms of news/entertainment broadcasting soon began to reach a global market. They also began to travel with us, via our smartphones, everywhere and all day long (the better for advertisers to track us and all of us to grow mildly or seriously obsessed). The new technology that makes the Internet and its contents possible has no intrinsic political bias to it; as already noted, neither the hardware nor the software of computers has any more natural relationship with democracy—despite early promises from its promoters—than with any other political form. But with its extraordinary scale, range, and ubiquity, the web has, in the parlance of Silicon Valley, been "disruptive," meaning an agent of change rather than stasis. And in the existing cultural and economic context, the Internet, and especially social media practices, have become particularly disruptive to those communicative norms that have long, at least in theory, been props to democracy. That includes not just traditional financial models for profiting off information but also moral-epistemic ones such as a commitment to veracity and honesty in expression, trust in expertise as well as fellow citizens, and adherence to a variety of institutional practices and rules related to speech. Facebook and its competitors have ended up, largely inadvertently but certainly with more impact than postmodernism, boosting post-truth currents within contemporary politics in much of the world. What that means is that social media has been another source inflaming the populist/expert dichotomy.

Some of the following arguments should sound familiar by now. First, social media organs like Facebook and Twitter have made it that much harder for the public to distinguish between truth, on the one hand, and opinion, advertisement, falsehood, or even wild speculation, on the other, distinctions long thought necessary for democracy to work. For the way these new digital platforms were designed, all of the above run together anarchically, with popularity as the only organizing principle. And in this profitable "wild west" climate, untruth seems increasingly to be gaining the upper hand.

Some false stories gain adherents and proliferate as a result of deliberate and organized disinformation campaigns that take advantage of search engine optimization and behavioral data collection (which exist in the first place to benefit marketing campaigns) to spread false news far and wide. The Russian government has clearly mastered this art in the last decade, using it all over the world to establish fake accounts and to spread fake stories to targeted recipients in a strategic effort to sow unrest. Other nations, including Iran and Saudi Arabia, along with fringe political groups and commercial interests, have done the same.

"Information warfare" is the new term for this form of international conflict with propaganda and lies at its core. But much of the time, ordinary, individual social media users make themselves into unconcerned or even unwitting conduits for various forms of phony news. That's the case whether the untruth starts from official sources on high or from the depths of the Internet. One 2018 study done by *Science* found that, on Twitter, falsehood and rumor dominate truth by every metric, reaching more people, penetrating deeper into social networks, and doing so more quickly than do accurate stories. Partly that's because the medium is designed to foster that which is provocative, which often means fantastic tales; platforms like Google literally help this happen by pushing sensational stories. It's also because the Internet reinforces the old lesson that exaggerations, selective reads, and even lies help us get attention and win arguments.[16] As the journalist Jack Holmes pointed out in 2017 in response to Trump circulating the unverified videos of a British hate group purportedly showing Muslims attacking white people, the president's falsehoods would not be nearly so dangerous if they were not attached to his "free-range access" to Twitter, best described as "a cesspool of unverified information and rampant hate," which allows him both to amplify his own lies and to spread others instantly and directly to 54 million followers, all of whom will potentially find reason to repeat them in some form despite the fact that they often know these tweets can't really be called true.[17] Even journalists will pass them along as part of their reporting of the day's events. Elsewhere in the world, as in Brazil, the messaging app WhatsApp has worked to the same effect for political leaders.[18] By these paths, falsehoods that were once given credence only on the far left or, more often, far right fringes of the political culture *can* enter the mainstream or, if they go "viral," take on a life of their own.

Furthermore, it isn't always clear to the average consumer what's what when it comes to social media postings. It has, for example, become increasingly difficult to tell the difference between legitimate and illegitimate polling data since even amateurs can now cheaply conduct their own polls using Google Surveys and then publish results without ever having to reveal their own names, their methods, or even who has been sampled.[19] Impostor accounts, issuing fake directives about topics like how to vote or why not to, are rampant too—and very hard to spot. Convincing fake video is, supposedly, just around the corner.[20] We are all likely, in other words, to be duped both as readers and as conveyers of this content. Social media companies like Facebook or search engines like Google, meanwhile, seem both unwilling and unable to impose any kind of order or even help us identify what's legitimate. That leaves factual truth, as required for democratic reasoning, largely indistinguishable from its many antonyms.

That also leads us to a second problem. Twitter, Facebook, and the like, by refusing to engage in any kind of vetting or quality control, end up diminishing further the authority of *all* forms of expertise. Instead, social media empowers ordinary individuals—in their capacity as, at once, content providers, readers, critics, publishers, and vigilante law-enforcement officers—to have full confidence in their own instincts and inclinations. The results have reshaped trust itself, decreasing it when it comes to established epistemic sources, from major press outlets to universities, and increasing it when it comes to oneself and one's cronies, with further consequences for the norms of democratic truth.

Some commentators claim this shift in the locus of authority constitutes a form of intellectual liberation (or at least they did until trolling became so prevalent). Not only can we make our own judgments about what to believe or share. Even more, it's sometimes argued that when we are online, without the veneer of social niceties, we can be more fully and candidly ourselves. We are freed, whether by the use of pseudonyms or by the distancing mechanism of the screen or both, to speak of ourselves and of others in a way that produces a kind of personal honesty—and allows us to choose as associates others who feel the same.

Yet it is increasingly clear that there is a flip side to this ethos of self-revelation and self-curation: excessive faith in one's own beliefs, coupled with suspicion of and even expressions of hostility toward all sources that result in unwelcome counterevidence or counterarguments as likely biased or venal, the once great sins of the nineteenth-century professional ethos. For in the end—and this is a third major problem—given both the vastness and the wildness of the Internet, the only way most of us can navigate its byways or even deal with our own social media accounts is not by seeking out a range of views but by creating ever-tighter "information bubbles." Which is to say, most of us end up deliberately amplifying the effects of the personalization algorithms that are designed to sell us products and retreating into siloes in which we largely engage only with our "friends," "followers," and those who, we can be sure, already share our values, tastes, and opinions. Then we block or lash out at all others as liars acting in bad faith.

Until recently, the great worry of media theorists was that the contemporary media landscape would end up being monopolized by a few big, powerful companies, like Sinclair Broadcasting in the United States or Berlusconi's holdings in Italy, leading de facto to a political and intellectual monoculture (which is what some media theorists already saw happening, under the workings of capitalism more generally, in the 1960s). And certainly these critics have not been altogether wrong; consider, for example, the fate of local newspapers and local reporting in all its previous diversity. But now, since the explosion of the Internet, something like the opposite has occurred, though with the same effect. Because we consumers have cheap access in the age of the Internet to such an overwhelming number of competing narratives, rife with so many competing facts *and* opinions, and stemming from so many sources, we still typically end up, if only to cope, retreating into insular, homogenous intellectual communities within its confines. The result is not just that people fail to garner the basic factual information needed for them to fulfill their role as citizens. Common ground—even the low-level shared realm of common sense necessary to start a meaningful conversation in the public sphere with a random interlocutor—becomes impossible to locate. Instead, say political theorists from Cass Sunstein to Nadia Urbinati, militant factionalism and extremism, bringing democratic dysfunction and the threat of violence with them, have become the characteristic political values of our time.[21]

It is hard to avoid the conclusion, then, that social media platforms, as profitable businesses with an outsized effect on all of our lives, encourage a kind of political disposition and behavior that may be fundamentally at odds with all that is necessary to anchor democratic governance. Internet-produced information bubbles, for example, can ultimately seem like an atavistic development; here is a case of new technology working to reproduce the culture of insular and even premodern villages, with their predilection for unfounded gossip and rumor mills as well as their demonization of enemies as tricksters and deceivers. Think, for example, about how false stories of child abductors spread in India recently via WhatsApp and ended in a trail of murders.[22] Or think of Facebook's vital role in the dissemination of vicious anti-Rohingya propaganda and lies that stoked the atrocities committed against the Muslim minority in Myanmar well before that country's leaders dismissed it all as fake news and jailed brave journalists who said otherwise.[23]

But when it comes to standards for truth, perhaps we have it backward. For it can also seem as if the basic tenets of the democratic imaginary, starting with the idea of a "free market" approach to speech, are not necessarily suited to the social and cultural conditions of today or that traditional ideals can no longer work the way they were once intended. One might even be tempted to conclude that some of these traditions are exacerbating our current problems, particularly as they relate to maintaining the delicate balance between popular knowledge and expertise.

Consider once again the First Amendment, added just after the completion of the U.S. Constitution. The federal government's largely laissez-faire approach to the realm of expression has remained vital in ensuring the possibility of unfettered dissent—Trump's venomous attacks on the press as "scum" and "sick people" and on kneeling football players' protesting police brutality as "sons of bitches" who "maybe . . . shouldn't be in the country" notwithstanding.[24] Yet the First Amendment was written for an information-poor world, not one characterized by information over-load and a massive competition for even a tiny bit of the public's attention. Moreover, American free-speech doc-trine, one of the most permissive such doctrines in the world, has proven essentially toothless when it comes to the fake news of today. Not only is the First Amendment of little aid in combatting incorrect facts (as Frederick Schauer points out, most twentieth-century American jurisprudence concerning speech rights has focused on advocacy, not description).[25] Freedom of expression has also been enlisted and weaponized as a practical tool in justifying the for-profit circulation of disinformation, as in the case of media platforms like WordPress' refusing to take down fake sites or fake ads or fake information. In addition, by shielding both abusive trolling and what are known as "flooding tactics" designed to manipulate what gets heard amidst all the online noise, this doctrine has enabled the silencing of unwelcome or unpopular voices, including disproportionately those of women and members of minority groups.[26] This is a new form of cen-sorship, or speech control, cleverly using free-speech doc-trine against itself.

Such techniques make it no longer necessary for quasi-authoritarian states to control the press or media outright by imposing formal restrictions on content or jailing dis-sident journalists; it is both easier and more effective to make the press a whipping boy, while also using it to one's advantage as a form of publicity. But even in more dem-ocratic environments, it is, at a minimum, becoming ever harder to remain convinced that the truth will emerge if we just let the so-called free market in information do its work without imposing any constraints, as Mill once imagined. What is popular with "customers" online, and thus attracts eyeballs and (even indirectly) money, rarely has much to do with what's either verifiable or serves democratic purposes.[27] The émigré philosopher Herbert Marcuse may have been right back in the 1960s when he said that, under such conditions, all talk of free speech becomes itself a cover for corrupt, inegalitarian, and antidemocratic practices.[28]

Mention of Marcuse also brings us back to where we left off in chapter 3. For in the end, economic realities—which abstract free-speech arguments traditionally ignore at all of our peril, as Marcuse noted fifty years ago—are as much responsible as anything else for the problems of truth in democracy down to this day. The point is not only that the information world is now, more than ever, dominated by globally powerful businesses like Google and WeChat *or* that in the United States big money has poured into shaping the political landscape, cementing "the unholy alliance of corrupt business and corrupt politics" (as Theodore Roosevelt put it in the last truly plutocratic age).[29] It is that the potential democratizing effects of the Internet in terms of knowledge accessibility and pluralism are proving meaningless given the chasms that have already left the winners and losers on the global stage existing in almost separate worlds. No wonder that tribalism now extends even to understandings of truth. The "post-truth" phenomenon that is roiling democracies around the world cannot be blamed on recent cultural and technological developments—postmodernism, new formats for political entertainment, social media, the weaponization of free speech—on their own. Rather, helped along by opportunistic political leaders and parties eager to gain advantages where they can, these factors have, to very varying degrees, exacerbated root causes that long predate the twenty-first century. That includes capitalism's failure to naturally promote democracy, which requires some commitment to stemming the tide of growing inequality within and among nations. And on a related note, that also includes the forces in democracies that pit expert truth against the prepolitical sense of "the people" rather them bringing them into concert.

So what, if anything, can be done? Can knowing either the deep or shallow history of the problem help us figure out how to get out of it? In one sense, no. History gives us little by way of precise lessons or answers—ever. More often it helps us to see the complexities, like the intersection of long- and short-term "causes" or the relationship between structure and contingency. But knowing more about the ideal ingredients of democratic truth, as well as its operational limitations over time, *can* potentially help get us started thinking about at least the broad parameters of a response.

To this end, let's turn one last time to Arendt, who showed with a few well-chosen examples picked out of the past that, at a minimum, when it comes to tackling the status of truth in politics, there are dangers associated both with doing too much and with doing too little. Reading *On Revolution,* Arendt's 1963 discussion of the French and American Revolutions, one quickly becomes convinced that efforts to cultivate and enforce total honesty and transparency in public life can only backfire, producing a climate of constant suspicion like that which ended in the

Reign of Terror in France in 1793–1794. Some tolerance for the arts of persuasion, manipulation, even hypocrisy as it veers into minor forms of lying turns out, paradoxically, to be essential to the practice of maintaining a politics committed to difference of opinion and agonism, as well as human rights protections—in short, liberal democracy.[30] But giving up on upholding *any* standards for truth, suggests Arendt in others of her writings, is also unacceptable as a public policy, since this approach is likely to snuff out even the possibility of democracy either as a form of political practice or as a theoretical commitment. Here we need only remember, as mentioned in chapter 3, the mid-twentieth-century totalitarian regimes of Stalin and Hitler, where the whole point of politics eventually became, according to Arendt, keeping alive the fantasy idea at their heart—and by any means possible, regardless of the effects on individual lives. Such are the extremes that we must strive to avoid.

To pursue or save any meaningful semblance of popular sovereignty along with human rights, the default strategy must, therefore, look different. The only seemingly viable solution becomes reinforcing by all means possible the more modest conception of truth in political life that started to take form in the late Enlightenment Atlantic world, but revised and adapted for the conditions of our own very different times. The trick will entail not just finding a way to cultivate pluralism, along with the cooperation of people from many walks of life and backgrounds as voters *and* as experts. A real solution will also require greater effort to locate that elusive balance point—equidistant from the technocratic temptation, on the one hand, and the populist one, on the other—that constitutes modern democracy's sweet spot, the point at which expert knowledge and popular sense can be imagined again as compensating for each other's limitations, and some low-level agreement about the state of the world can provide a foundation for vigorous debate.

But where to start? Any countereffort likely requires tackling the problem of truth head on, as well as indirectly. The necessary, even if insufficient, first step may be to constantly encourage, within our new media landscape, small-bore ways of modeling (without legislating) truth-telling and lie-detecting as epistemological and ethical commitments in public life. That is, they need first to be reinforced as a fundamental form of democratic practice.

At the most basic and banal level, we require journalists and all those who act as professional communicators to continue to seek out and disseminate empirically sound, carefully verified information—the kind most vital to democratic deliberation—and to do so in a "plain" or blunt, but not defamatory, idiom. Sometimes that will mean, as in the case of the Soviet journalist Arseny Roginsky, working despite the risks and in defiance of the authorities to "rescue from oblivion all those historical facts and names that are currently doomed to perish or disappear," as the underground journal that he published in the Soviet Union in the 1980s put it.[31] Sometimes that will mean simply adding to the historical record, documenting what *truly* happened, which is what every current *New York Times* ad campaign likes to remind us is what investigative journalists in a flourishing democracy do.

Either way, the point becomes pursuing the truth, by means of the most scrupulous methods and standards of evidence of one's profession, wherever it might lead.

Reporting should not be partisan. But we also don't need, in the name of "balance," fairness, or neutrality, to reopen settled debates about the flatness of the earth or the ethics of chattel slavery; there is little positive value in giving airtime to claims that have no legitimacy in the present from either a scholarly and empirical or popular moral perspective. The goal should remain objectivity, however compromised it is as a concept now, but understood as encompassing well-documented anecdotal evidence attentive to values and affect, as well as facts and figures. Moreover, those who relay information must make an effort to do so in a clear-eyed, precise idiom that, in the words of novelist Chimamanda Ngozi Adichie, "call[s] things what they actually are" rather than trades in obscurity or euphemism.[32] These are all strategies with old pedigrees.

On the flip side—and here again this applies to all those engaged in political communication, including investigative journalists but also career politicians—it remains important to expose errors and falsehoods in a dry and decisive but also unrelenting fashion. For it is essential, even if it fails to persuade all comers, that those who are interested in preserving some standards for truth claims also commit to bringing to light damaging falsehoods, especially of the factual variety, and to documenting them for posterity as well as the present. This is where journalists have recently also been vital, whether that has meant calling out the American president's lies on a daily basis or exposing the falsity of popular conspiracy theories. So have fact-checkers at dedicated fact-checking sites like Snopes, Politifact, FactCheck.org (as well as their international counterparts) who have provided an exhaustive running log of what can and cannot be verified in the contemporary public sphere. They too have directly helped, in a tradition that runs from Kant to Ida B. Wells, to keep visible those lines between truth and its antagonists, visual and verbal alike, that the Internet so often makes hazy.

Surely, media giants could do more to help maintain these distinctions too, even if it runs counter to their bottom line. It's high time to keep up the pressure on Facebook, WhatsApp, and their competitors to find better technical solutions to solve the problem of disinformation campaigns, whether that involves shutting down phony sites and removing phony information from circulation or simply tagging them as false for readers. Better cybersecurity would help. So would different algorithms that do not privilege the worst information out there in the first place. Can we hope that researchers at the Full Fact firm in London will actually succeed in developing what they are calling a real-time "bullshit detector"?[33] This too would likely be a rudimentary but useful first step.

Then there is the First Amendment in the United States and other free-speech constitutional clauses elsewhere, most of which are quite different in scope but standard issue since the eighteenth century for all liberal democratic nations. This is hardly the time to ditch them. As David Cole recently pointed out in the *New York Review of Books,* a wide area of protection for dissenting speech becomes even more essential in moments when hostility to civil liberties and the manufacturing of official propaganda are on the rise. We would be foolhardy to trust legislatures or presidents any more than corporations in determining what should be said or heard.[34] But must that translate into free-speech absolutism, or the right to say anything, including hateful or false utterances, with weapons gleaming in the background (as in the neo-Nazi rally in Charlottesville, Virginia, in 2017), or with disregard for the potentially pernicious effects on the lives of the people in question (as in the Alex Jones/Infowars claims about staged deaths in the Newtown, Connecticut school shootings), or without concern for the fate of the previous speaker him- or herself (as in everyday online trolling that silences through threats of violence or humiliation)? It may well be time to consider modifying free speech laws to limit the damage that free speech can do. At the very least, there may be compelling state interest—including the safeguarding of democracy—in regulations that would bring the literal market in information in today's "attention economy" more in line with the ideal speech forum imagined long ago by legal theorist Alexander Meiklejohn and others.

The law might, for example, be used to put pressure on social media companies, as in Europe after the Brexit vote, to make sure that the algorithms they employ are neither preventing us from hearing less powerful voices that we would benefit from having access to nor giving megaphones to those we have good reason to believe are hurting the social fabric by spreading dangerous forms of hate and disinformation or engaging in harassment. This isn't easy terrain. In the United States, *Buckley v. Valeo* (1976) is often cited to the effect that "the concept that government may restrict the speech of some elements of society in order to enhance the relative voice of others is wholly foreign to the First Amendment."[35] And Facebook's Mark Zuckerberg, when he recently stumbled over questions about his company's stance on the posting of the lie of

Holocaust denial, made clear both how little his company is prepared to deal with these issues and how difficult they are to get right, especially since American law is something of an outlier on this point.[36] But as the legal scholar Tim Wu has been arguing lately, given changes in technology and politics globally, it may be time to demand new laws or regulations that would require our major speech platforms to behave as public trustees, with an obligation to promote a robust and tolerant speech environment when it comes to matters of public concern.[37]

Still, neither bold-facing truth and putting it into plain, simple words in all our media outlets nor tinkering with free-speech laws to eliminate certain kinds of inflammatory untruths will alone save democracy or honesty or even knowledge (even if subscriptions to Pro Publica and the *New York Times* have soared as acts of "resistance" since the election of Trump). It is precisely because democracy is always an unfinished project, rooted in protection for plural *doxai,* that strategies for tackling the shaky status of truth today are going to require more than newspapers, websites, broadcasts, podcasts, and "feeds" all devoted to facts—especially when facts themselves have become suspect. A wide range of institutions, themselves founded in part to help us police the boundaries between truth and falsehood as a civic responsibility, need reinforcement and, in some cases, serious modification. That goes well beyond just the press, for the number of formal institutions important to the communicative and epistemological dimension of politics has vastly expanded since the eighteenth century. The key is to find ways to support these institutions—and their attendant formal processes for establishing and conveying factual truth—that also encourage rather than thwart popular participation in politics (since it is also possible to use democratic institutions to kill off democracy from the inside) and do so with respect for pluralism, especially when it comes to experiences and values. The goal of democracy has to remain truth without dogmatism if democracy is to have any meaning at all.

That starts with protecting the integrity of elections, one of the cornerstones of democracy, as expressions of something called the "popular will" and, ideally, reflective of all peoples across differences of income, race, gender, religion, or any other particulars. Democracy fails when some people are, without legitimate reason, de facto or de jure disenfranchised. It also fails when elections are either rigged or perceived to be—hence the particular dangers associated with demagogues' frequent false claims of illegitimacy or cheating when the vote count goes against them. To combat post-truth as a symptom or cause of the deterioration of democracy, voting must be secured as a fundamental right (which means working not to purge the rolls but to expand them, possibly by adding residents as well as citizens) and encouraged as a critical civic responsibility, if not requirement. Voting systems then need to be made safe from hacking or other nefarious actions on the part of self-interested parties. And the distorting influence of money on what voters read and see up to the moment they vote must be reduced, in part because of questions of equity and in part because we know how much it warps the kind of open public conversation about both values and truths that a legitimate election requires as a precursor. In France, President Macron has spent part of 2018 pushing a bill that would allow judges to block content deemed fake during the three months before an election.[38] Such a bill would now have no chance of passing the First Amendment test in the United States. But it does suggest that we in the United States and elsewhere need to think long and hard about the pitfalls of allowing a fully free-market approach, where money is unlimited, to shape the business of arriving at the consensual "serviceable truths" or "political truths" that democratic elections are supposed to help produce. Here too enhanced rules and regulations for communication are required if truth is to be either the starting point of our political process or the aim.

Supporting an independent judiciary, another eighteenth-century innovation, is thus also vital in this task. And that's not only because the court system remains essential (despite many recent decisions to the contrary as of late) to defending so many of our civil liberties, from the right of the press to publish criticism of the government to the right of citizens to vote in the first place. It is also because it is courts of law that are, in principle, in the business of upholding the reign of truthfulness, as opposed to falsehood or deception, in all our public spaces, from the trading floors of Wall Street, to the halls of Congress, to the interiors of courtrooms themselves. Following legal procedure in courtrooms, ordinary and exalted people alike are asked, under oath, to share information whose accuracy and veracity will then be weighed by a judge or a jury of their peers, as well as, sometimes, the court of public opinion. We all know that politics (personal and ideological) is unavoidable in much of this and that judges, despite Chief Justice John Roberts's famous claims to the contrary, do not really act like baseball umpires at all; the law turns on the kinds of facts that cannot be so easily separated from interpretation, which also means values and judgments. Witness the recent Supreme Court confirmation hearing of (then) appeals court judge Brett Kavanaugh in which the judge's own account of his past, not to mention his overall veracity, read differently depending on one's prior political convictions.[39] But more broadly, the legal system—and faith in its processes to discover and punish forms of deception regardless of their place of origin—remains essential to enforcing the idea that striving for something called "the truth" is, at once, an epistemological and an ethical obligation in our lives in common.[40]

Schools, colleges, and universities, public and private, play an equally critical role in this business. The point is not only that schools of all kinds and levels are where established truths are passed along to the young, but also that institutions formally dedicated to teaching and research are, both by accident and by design, places where particular "regimes of truth" take shape. For Foucault, that made schooling a frequently nefarious business. But schools and universities, even as we recognize them as often undemocratic and coercive spaces, also provide us with a special opportunity to instill the epistemic-moral aspirations essential to fostering a truly democratic truth culture.

Starting in elementary school and continuing until the end of their formal educations, students in a democracy should be taught just *how* scholars come to legitimate, verifiable knowledge: what, for example, counts as trustworthy evidence? or a well-reasoned argument? or a testable hypothesis? Students also need opportunities to try their hand at creating such knowledge for themselves, building on existing authoritative truths and applying different disciplinary methods. But I'd argue that teachers' energies have, at the same time, also to run in reverse: to showing students how to distinguish truth from unverified belief, hunches, wishes, or tall tales, and to encouraging them to practice a healthy skepticism (which is not the same as paranoia) about verities of all kinds. Ideally, children and young adults will also discover how one might begin to refine or even dismantle obsolete truths, even as they also learn to practice tolerance for alternative points of view.[41] After all, sensibly questioning the veracity of received wisdom, the objectivity of institutions or processes for the transmission of knowledge, the sincerity of political and business elites when it comes to the motives behind their utterances, and even the legitimacy of expert claims to disinterested professionalism is closely linked to the practice of emancipatory democracy too.

Along these lines, conventional wisdom today says that the sciences—natural, physical, and even the quantitative social sciences like economics—are especially good for teaching effective truth practices. That is surely right to a degree. But just as much, we might (unfashionably) think about stressing the humanities and, especially, history. Historians of all kinds depend on the existence of facts. Even those most taken with postmodernism do not accept that there is no such thing as an untruth or argue that it is the same to make it all up as to build on verified documentation. Yet historical facts are, as we have established, also the kinds of basic truths that are most easy to manipulate and also often the most politically sensitive and contested. That's why Truth Commissions have, since the 1980s, been established all over the globe, from postdictatorship Chile and Peru, to postapartheid South Africa, to contemporary American universities grappling with their own racist pasts. The idea behind them all is that, in order to come to terms with prior political violence and to begin the process of finding some basic consensus on which to build, the public needs an opportunity to collect and hear the (often conflicting) evidence of experience, or a kind of lived truth, from all sides, including those that have previously gone unheard. For only with this exposure, no matter how uncomfortable it may be, can a new, truly democratic national or local narrative be forged.[42] There is a lesson here for all efforts to construct accounts of what *really* happened.

However, that's not all that history's good for. For what historians, like their colleagues in literature, art, and philosophy, actually teach—and which is equally vital as a form of training—is not just "what are the facts" and "where do we find them." They teach interpretation. That means learning how to read and to analyze for meaning. It also means grasping the complexity of any form of truth beyond the most elemental, from how a policy can simultaneously hurt some people and help others, to how complex truths can themselves look so different to two people who hail from the same place. This is ultimately how students learn how to be citizens: people who understand what came before but who can also weigh and consider alternate visions of the future.

Support for a democratic truth regime should thus also lead us to uphold and encourage a tradition of nonviolent (but not necessarily "civil" in the sense of polite) protest, a tradition that well predates modern democracy but that had a real revival in the 1960s and into the 1970s across much of the world. Such protests put people in the streets, largely apart from formal institutions and their speech rules, offering critiques but also applying pressure on them to reform their ways. Citizens can and should again join forces to protest *against* forms of lying and corruption as ethical violations. Citizens should also seize the opportunity to agitate publicly *for* revised and updated methods and standards of truth determination now that epistemology has reemerged as a critical political battleground. Getting cops to wear cameras that accurately record their interactions with civilians, and especially black civilians, is one recent successful outcome of demonstrations of this sort orchestrated by the grassroots organization Black Lives Matter.[43] The 2017 March for Science, which took shape in response to the seeming anti-science bent of the early days of the Trump administration, is another. It has now morphed into an organization that supports rallies around the globe designed to convey the message that "science is real" (as protestors in Oklahoma put it) and that we need "evidence-based policy that serves all communities" (according to the organization's homepage).[44] This is one place where experts and citizens should also find common purpose.

And one could go one step further too. As Mahatma Gandhi made clear in the very different context of late-colonial India, truth, or *satya*, is ultimately both the condition and the consequence of all politics. Action is political in the positive sense only insofar as it challenges or disturbs ordinary, conventional understandings of the world and ultimately reveals the truth beneath the surface, changing self-conceptions in the process.[45] Truth-seeking and truth-telling are, in other words, inextricably linked to all liberation movements as well.

Yet there is a final risk here. All this pro-truth evangelizing and reinforcement of various democratic traditions might well ultimately be moot if we remain totally divided from one another by every material or psychic measure. Pierre Rosanvallon, writing recently about strategies for combating populism in France, proposed that, in the end, what matters is that people from all walks of life possess a shared language of politics, a common platform for starting a wide-ranging conversation.[46] Arendt, our intermittent guide through this tricky terrain, would probably have agreed. Neither, though, has much to say about if or how such a thing could be possible in a world defined so thoroughly by economic inequality and stratification as the present one. Could empirically minded, plain-speaking, fact-checking journalists, bulked-up suffrage, court and educational systems, a tradition of street demonstrations, and the development of a new kind of First Amendment jurisprudence that paid more attention to maintaining facticity and reversing silencing techniques be enough to revitalize the democratic take on truth? Could *any* of the elements of the democratic imaginary, including liberty, equality, and dignity as well as truth (all of which Trump and his counterparts have conspicuously ignored or rejected), become, once again, a widely shared goal? It is hard to say yes to either question as long as people seem to be living in such different worlds, economically and psychologically.

There are, of course, no direct lines between economic hardship and any particular ideological position. Places around the world hard hit by the downturn of 2008 have today placed in power very varied kinds of leaders and parties, alone and in coalitions. Even in the United States, household income, as opposed to geography or cultural identifiers, is generally a poor indicator of voting preferences. That's because so much of politics today is about questions of identity, lifestyle, and respect, unconnected to pocketbooks (something the very wealthy have, in different ways, encouraged across party lines). Nevertheless, to reach a consensus about what constitutes truth requires agreeing in some minimal way about what reality looks like and, even more, how we can know or represent this reality and why it matters—ethically, epistemologically, politically—how we do so. That's going to be difficult when not even schools or the military provide for a common experience across economic differences and when money seems to create distinctions in almost every aspect of American life, including perceptions, trust, and the rest. All of which makes one wonder if the preservation of the democratic conception of truth will not ultimately require a considerably more substantive fix.

From the right, the answer lies in part in efforts to bolster a more culturally and, sometimes, ethnically homogenous world. But the left has a traditional answer too: a turn away from our reigning political-economic principles and toward a world in which, thanks to better redistributive policies, the extremes simply aren't so far apart. Or, to put it slightly differently, it's time again to think about alternatives to the logic of "the market always knows best" when we consider living standards as well as the pursuit of truth. For in the end, the story of modern democracy remains also the story of modern capitalism, and any real solution to our current ills probably requires addressing them in tandem.

Otherwise, we may be left with only technocracy, with its liberal but anti-egalitarian, managerial ethos, on the one hand, and populism, with its demophilic but homogenizing, anti-intellectual cast and disinterest in most constitutional rights, on the other, duking it out to the bitter end. Without a continuing commitment to the messy business of good-faith negotiation starting and ending with undogmatic truth, the democratic imaginary that is essential to sustaining democracy in practice seems doomed.

Most forms of truth, even undogmatic truth, can probably do fine without the existence of democracy, just as they did before and still do in many places. Voltaire counted not on a republic but on an enlightened monarch as the best hope to protect and encourage the pursuit of real knowledge. And today, science flourishes in various parts of the world that can't be called democracies. Popular participation in scientific or even social scientific research is, in any case, minimal everywhere. Dewey's old analogy has some serious flaws.

Surely, though, democracy—a form of representative government whose prevalence globally has increased dramatically from the 1970s until quite recently, when the momentum has started to go in the other direction—cannot survive without any commitment to verifiable truth and truth-telling from either the population at large or the powers on high. At a practical level, a basic commitment to truth-telling or veracity as a moral position is central to maintaining the interpersonal trust that democracy, in its modern incarnation, needs to be effective. That much was clear already in the eighteenth century, before the Age of Revolutions even began. So was the necessity of sound information or factual truth; democratic debate is premised from the start on every opinion being informed by some shared body of facts. But even more, we've seen that the pursuit of truth is vital in a democracy in an abstract way: as a key aspiration. Democracy depends not on having universal knowledge or the ability to name and explain everything that reality encompasses but, rather, on the idea that all this debate and deliberation will ultimately lead to larger, if still collaborative and contingent, truths that will, in turn, benefit humankind as a whole. Truth is a necessary horizon for political life right along with liberty and equality and happiness. It may even be more foundational. That idea is what, in good part, keeps the possibility of democracy going—and that may be why it matters most.

But do we still need that old idea we continue to call democracy? Some people might look around and conclude, the political theorist Wendy Brown points out in a recent book, that the fate of democracy should be the least of our worries today. The planet as a whole is failing. People all over the globe live in misery. Deliberation, voting rights, or constitutional protections are, in this context, *not* what is most at stake. Indeed, some might even say that democratic discourse, for all its talk of equality and liberty and justice for all, is, generally, a particularly pernicious mask, a way of papering over exclusion, domination, and injustice. Truth could well be one more mythology covering for something else—a position Brown herself comes close to endorsing on occasion.[47]

Democracy has, though, the extraordinary virtue of always providing for the possibility of second chances. That's precisely because of its theoretical (and longstanding) relationship to a particular vision of truth. By this way of thinking, democracy's great advantage is not a question of the empirical outcomes it generates, as some theorists today would have it. Rather, it is that we can never be certain we've got it right, and that's okay. New information or new knowledge can, at any point, potentially lead to new plans with new people at the helm. Moreover, knowing this is vital. For it is only if we can imagine moral and epistemological progress—that is, progress away from lies and propaganda and toward a truer view of reality, however elusive—that we can begin to rectify the gaps between theory and practice, between democratic ideals and the world in which we actually live and operate now.

On the one hand, this book has been designed to illustrate just how multifaceted and also delicate is the truth construct on which democracy was reconstructed in the Enlightenment and Age of Revolutions. Another purpose has been to show how precarious this relationship has remained ever since—and how easily it might erode or be pushed into authoritarianism of one kind or another by oligarchical experts or a tyrannical majority or even a dictator or demagogue. It is hard to resist here drawing attention to Weimar Germany, the brief democratic interlude between World War I and the Third Reich, when a confluence of media attacks on the legitimacy of the new government reinforced by lies, a growing separation between urban and rural culture, a conservative movement willing to align itself with illiberal forces for expediency, and severe economic dislocation together produced a loss of faith in the possibility of democratic progress that was broad enough to bring antidemocratic forces legally to the fore. But, on the other hand, looking at the present in a historical framework also offers a modest form of hope. It demonstrates that we humans can make collective choices that can shape what happens next. That's sometimes called agency. In the end, truth, like democracy, isn't something that simply exists in the world. It is, rather, something that we must always consciously and collectively forge.

Notes

Introduction

1. William A. Galston, "Truth and Democracy: Theme and Variations," in *Truth and Democracy*, ed. Jeremy Elkins and Andrew Norris (Philadelphia: University of Pennsylvania Press, 2011), 144.

Chapter 1

1. Gideon Resnick, "How Pro-Trump Twitter Bots Spread Fake News," *Daily Beast,* November 17, 2016, https://www.thedailybeast.com/how-pro-trump-twitter-bots-spread-fake-news?ref=scroll; and Oliver Roeder, "Why We're Sharing 3 Million Russian Troll Tweets," *FiveThirtyEight,* July 31, 2018, https://fivethirtyeight.com/features/why-were-sharing-3-million-russian-troll-tweets/. Something similar happened in the United Kingdom in the buildup to Brexit, as a British Parliamentary commission has established beyond a doubt: Carole Cadwalladr, "'Plucky Little Panel' That Found the Truth about Fake News, Facebook and Brexit," *Guardian,* July 28, 2018, https://www.theguardian.com/politics/2018/jul/28/dcms-committee-report-finds-truth-fake-news-facebook-brexit.

2. Daniel Arkin and Ben Popken, "How the Internet's Conspiracy Theories Turned Parkland Students into 'Crisis Actors,'" *NBC News,* February 21, 2018, https://www.nbcnews.com/news/us-news/how-internet-s-conspiracy-theorists-turned-parkland-students-crisis-actors-n849921.

3. Henry J. Farrell and Rick Perlstein, "Our Hackable Political Future," *New York Times,* February 4, 2018, https://www.nytimes.com/2018/02/04/opinion/hacking-politics-future.html.

4. Glenn Kessler and Meg Kelly, "President Trump Has Made More Than 2,000 False or Misleading Claims over 355 Days," *Washington Post,* January 10, 2018, https://www.washingtonpost.com/news/fact-checker/wp/2018/01/10/president-trump-has-made-more-than-2000-false-or-misleading-claims-over-355-days/?noredirect=on&utm_term=.295833bcbdea. Since the start of the Trump presidency, the mainstream press has used the words "untruth" and "falsehood" increasingly frequently in reporting on the president, backed up by the claim that it is possible to objectively detail an escalation in the circulation of deliberate misstatements over the Bush or Obama administrations; the *Washington Post* does not, however, use the word "lie," and the *New York Times* uses it sparingly, preferring other terms.

5. Susan Glasser, "It's True: Trump Is Lying More, and He's Doing It on Purpose," *New Yorker,* August 3, 2018, https://www.newyorker.com/news/letter-from-trumps-washington/trumps-escalating-war-on-the-truth-is-on-purpose.

6. See Sara Boboltz, "Trump Says It's OK He Misled Media about Son's Russia Meeting [in Trump Tower in 2016]," *Huffington Post.* June 15, 2018, https://www.huffingtonpost.com/entry/trump-donald-trump-jr-statement_us_5b23be85e4b0d4fc01fda677.

7. Xavier Marquez, "This Is Why Authoritarian Leaders Use the 'Big Lie,'" *Washington Post,* January 26, 2017, https://www.washingtonpost.com/news/monkey-cage/wp/2017/01/26/this-is-why-authoritarian-leaders-use-the-big-lie/?utm_term=.a2394b303bc9. See too Harry Frankfurt, *On Bullshit* (Princeton, NJ: Princeton University Press, 2005) on the kinds of lies that are primarily about manipulation or getting the effects one wants, not covering up the truth.

8. See Craig Calhoun, "The Big Picture: Trump's Attack on Knowledge," *Public Books,* November 29, 2017, http://www.publicbooks.org/the-big-picture-trumps-attack-on-knowledge/. More specifically, see Paul Voosen, "Trump White House Quietly Cancels NASA Research Verifying Greenhouse Gas Cuts," *Science,* May 9, 2018,

http://www.sciencemag.org/news/2018/05/trump-white-house
-quietly-cancels-nasa-research-verifying-greenhouse-gas-cuts.

9. Much of this evidence is anecdotal, but see too, for example, Andrew Arenge, John Lipinski, and Ashley Tallevi, "Poll: Republicans Who Think Trump Is Untruthful Still Approve of Him," *NBC News*, May 2, 2018, https://www.nbcnews.com/politics /politics-news/poll-republicans-who-think-trump-untruthful-still -approve-him-n870521, which showed that at the time of publication, 76 percent of Republicans believed Trump told the truth "all or most of the time," and 22 percent said he told the truth only "some of the time or less"; but 56 percent of the latter group "still approve of his work as president."

10. See Steve Coll, "The Distrust That Trump Relies Upon," *New Yorker*, December 22, 2017, https://www.newyorker.com /news/daily-comment/the-distrust-that-trump-relies-upon, which details the results of a Gallup poll on the declining confidence in the country's chief institutions, excluding the police and military. On the stronger effect on the right, see Matthew Rozsa, "A Majority of Republicans Now Say 'Media Is the Enemy of the People,'" *Salon*, April 27, 2018, https://www.salon.com/2018/04/27 /a-majority-of-republicans-now-say-media-is-the-enemy-of-the -people/, though the author points out that voters overall trust the media more than the president. Also see the Pew survey of 2017 that showed 58 percent of Republicans believe "colleges are having a negative effect on the ways things are going in the country," as cited in Jennifer Agiesta, "Poll: Party Divisions Extend to Impression of Higher Education," CNN, July 10, 2017, https://www.cnn .com/2017/07/10/politics/college-media-party-poll/index.html. Conversely, see Emily Shugerman, "Trump Supporters Share More Fake News Than Anyone Else, Study Shows," *Independent*, February 7, 2018, https://www.independent.co.uk/news/world/americas /us-politics/trump-supporters-share-more-fake-news-junk-news -oxford-study-a8199056.html, which cites an Oxford University study showing that more unsubstantiated or misleading "junk" news about politics, economics, and culture was shared on Facebook and Twitter by Trump supporters than by all other kinds of American audiences put together.

11. David Roberts, "Donald Trump and the Rise of Tribal Epistemology," *Vox*, May 19, 2017, https://www.vox.com/policy-and -politics/2017/3/22/14762030/donald-trump-tribal-epistemology. See also Roberts, "America Is Facing an Epistemic Crisis," *Vox*, November 2, 2017, https://www.vox.com/policy-and-politics/2017 /11/2/16588964/america-epistemic-crisis.

12. Al Gore, *An Inconvenient Truth* (Emmaus, PA: Rodale Press, 2006), was released in conjunction with a 2006 documentary film with the same name. Max Weber, in "Science as a Vocation" (1917), refers to "inconvenient facts" as ones that are inconvenient for "party opinions."

13. Mattathias Schwartz, "'Facts Are in the Eye of the Beholder,' Says Roger Stone, Trump Confidant," *The Intercept*, March 6, 2017, https://theintercept.com/2017/03/06/facts-are-in -the-eye-of-the-beholder-says-roger-stone-trump-confidante-in -exclusive-interview/.

14. On the characteristics of this rhetoric, see Kathleen Hall Jamieson and Doron Taussig, "Disruption, Demonization, Deliverance, and Norm Destruction: The Rhetorical Signature of Donald J. Trump," *Political Science Quarterly* 132, no. 4 (winter 2017–2018): 619–50. On these survey results, see Amy B. Wang, "'Post-truth' Named 2016 Word of the Year by Oxford Dictionaries," *Washington Post*, November 16, 2016, https://www.washingtonpost.com/news /the-fix/wp/2016/11/16/post-truth-named-2016-word-of-the-year -by-oxford-dictionaries/?noredirect=on, which cited a *Washington Post*-ABC News tracking poll just before the 2016 presidential election that found Trump was considered more honest than Clinton by an eight-point margin.

15. See Griff Witte, "Once Fringe Soros Conspiracy Theory Takes Center Stage in Hungarian Election," *Washington Post*, March 17, 2018, https://www.washingtonpost.com/world /europe/once-fringe-soros-conspiracy-theory-takes-center-stage -in-hungarian-election/2018/03/17/f0a1d5ae-2601-11e8 -a227-fd2b009466bc_story.html?noredirect=on&utm_term= .81896afba6fb. Also see Judith Vonberg, "George Soros Foundation Leaves Hungary Amid Government Crackdown," CNN, May

16, 2018, https://www.cnn.com/2018/05/15/europe/george-soros
-foundation-leaves-hungary-intl/index.html.

16. Hannah Beech, "'No Such Thing as Rohingya': Myanmar
Erases a History," *New York Times*, December 2, 2017, https://www
.nytimes.com/2017/12/02/world/asia/myanmar-rohingya-denial
-history.html; and Joshua Kurlantzick, "Why Aung San Suu Kyi
Isn't Protecting the Rohingya in Burma," *Washington Post*, September 15, 2017, https://www.washingtonpost.com/outlook/why-aung
-san-suu-kyi-isnt-protecting-the-rohingya-in-burma/2017/09/15
/c88b10fa-9900-11e7-87fc-c3f7ee4035c9_story.html?utm_term=
.071d6a08ce5e.

17. Steve Peoples, "Bloomberg Warns of 'Epidemic of Dishonesty,'" AP News, May 12, 2018, https://apnews.com/e21ff1230098
479a9d17737b64ebbc74.

18. Hannah Arendt, "Lying in Politics: Reflections on the Pentagon Papers" (1971), in *Crises of the Republic* (New York: Mariner
Books, 1972), 4. On the larger question of the prevalence and ethics
of lying in political life, see Martin Jay, *The Virtues of Mendacity: On
Lying in Politics* (Charlottesville: University of Virginia Press, 2010);
Lionel Cliffe, Maureen Ramsay, et al., *The Politics of Lying: Implications for Democracy* (New York: Palgrave Macmillan, 2000); and
Sophia Rosenfeld, "Liehards," *Nation*, September 10, 2012, 27–30.

19. On historians' telling us recently there has always been fake
news, see, for example, Kevin Young, *Bunk: The Rise of Hoaxes,
Humbug, Plagiarists, Phonies, Post-Facts and Fake News* (Minneapolis: Graywolf Press, 2017); Jacob Soll, "The Long and Brutal
History of Fake News," *Politico*, December 18, 2016, https://www
.politico.com/magazine/story/2016/12/fake-news-history-long
-violent-214535; and David Uberti, "The Real History of Fake
News," *Columbia Journalism Review* (December 16, 2016), https://
www.cjr.org/special_report/fake_news_history.php. Especially on
early modern France, see Robert Zaretsky, "Fake News Spreading Like Wildfire? The French Had the Problem Before We Did,"
Los Angeles Times, December 18, 2016, http://www.latimes.com
/opinion/op-ed/la-oe-zaretsky-fake-news-france-libelle-20161218
-story.html; and Robert Darnton, "The True History of Fake News,"

NYRB Daily, February 13, 2017, https://www.nybooks.com/daily /2017/02/13/the-true-history-of-fake-news/.

20. See Marvin Perry and Frederick M. Schweitzer, eds., *Antisemitic Myths: A Historical and Contemporary Anthology* (Bloomington: Indiana University Press, 2008).

21. See Niraj Chokshi, "'Crisis Actor' Isn't a New Smear. The Idea Goes Back to the Civil War Era," *New York Times,* February 24, 2018, https://www.nytimes.com/2018/02/24/us/crisis-actors-florida -shooting.html. There is, of course, also a history of real "false flag" narratives as well.

22. George Washington, original draft of his "Farewell Address" (1796), cited in Patrick Novotny, *The Press in American Politics, 1787–2012* (Santa Barbara, CA: Praeger, 2014), 14–15.

23. See Lorraine Daston and Peter Galison, *Objectivity* (New York: Zone Books, 2007).

24. See, in addition to "Lying in Politics," Arendt's slightly earlier essay "Truth and Politics" (1967), in *Between Past and Future: Eight Exercises in Political Thought* (New York: Viking, 1968); and on the meaning of both, Sophia Rosenfeld, "On Lying: Writing Philosophical History after the Enlightenment and after Arendt," in *The Worlds of American Intellectual History,* ed. Joel Isaac et al. (New York: Oxford University Press, 2017), esp. 220–24.

25. The list includes Sheldon Rampton and John Stauber, *Weapons of Mass Deception: The Uses of Propaganda in Bush's War on Iraq* (2003); David Corn, *The Lies of George W. Bush: Mastering the Politics of Deception* (2003); Nicholas von Hoffman, *Hoax: Why Americans Are Suckered by White House Lies* (2004); Paul Waldman, *Fraud: The Strategy behind the Bush Lies and Why the Media Didn't Tell You* (2004); Al Franken, *Lies and the Lying Liars Who Tell Them: A Fair and Balanced Look at the Right* (2003); and Joe Conason, *Big Lies: The Right-Wing Propaganda Machine and How It Distorts the Truth* (2003).

26. The term "post-truth" was first used by Steve Tesich in a January 1992 article in the *Nation* about the Reagan years entitled "A Government of Lies." It was used again by Ralph Keyes in *The Post-Truth Era: Dishonesty and Deception in Contemporary Life* (2004). But its takeoff as a term has been since 2015, leading the *OED* to

define it as "relating to or denoting circumstances in which objective facts are less influential in shaping public opinion than appeals to emotion and personal belief" and to name it as the word of the year in 2016, before the election results were known in the United States but after the Brexit vote in the United Kingdom; see Wang, "Post-truth Named 2016 Word of the Year by Oxford Dictionaries."

27. Arendt, "Truth in Politics," 239.

28. See Bernard Williams, *Truth and Truthfulness: An Essay in Genealogy* (Princeton, NJ: Princeton University Press, 2002).

29. On the clear, realist position that there is a reality independent of us and how that means some questions—like was Louis XVI decapitated—actually have "right" answers, see Errol Morris, "Is There Such a Thing as Truth," *Boston Review*, April 30, 2018, http://bostonreview.net/politics/errol-morris-there-such-thing-truth.

30. Simon Blackburn neatly summarizes in *Truth: A Guide* (Oxford: Oxford University Press, 2005), xvii, that one can be an absolutist about the nature of truth and a skeptic about the possession of truth. This is another version of Bernard Williams's claim in *Truth and Truthfulness* that while human attitudes toward truth and conceptions of knowledge have a history rife with variability, truth itself does not; see 61–62. Philip Kitcher, in *Science, Truth, and Democracy* (New York: Oxford University Press, 2001), calls this position "modest realism."

31. See Michel Foucault, "Truth and Power," in *Power/Knowledge: Selected Interviews and Other Writings, 1972–1977,* ed. Colin Gordon (New York: Pantheon, 1980), 109–33, see 133. It is worth noting that even as Foucault insisted that truth was more produced than discovered, he never denied the existence of facts or reduced knowledge to nothing but power (despite the claims of his many critics). See too Karl Mannheim's earlier arguments for the socially situated nature of what counts in any given moment as knowledge, in *Ideology and Utopia: An Introduction to the Sociology of Knowledge* (1936).

32. See, for example, Peter Dear, "From Truth to Disinterestedness in the Seventeenth Century," *Social Studies of Science* 22, no. 4 (1992): 619–31; and Barbara Shapiro, *Probability and Certainty in Seventeenth-Century England: A Study of the Relationships between Natural Science, Religion, History, Law and Literature* (Princeton, NJ:

Princeton University Press, 1983) and *A Culture of Fact: England, 1550–1720* (Ithaca, NY: Cornell University Press, 2003).

33. Lying too has its historians—see Perez Zagorin, *Ways of Lying: Dissimulation, Persecution and Conformity in Early Modern Europe* (Cambridge, MA: Harvard University Press, 1990); and Dallas Denery, *The Devil Wins: A History of Lying from the Garden of Eden to the Enlightenment* (Princeton, NJ: Princeton University Press, 2015)—as do error and ignorance, as in Robert Proctor and Londa Schiebinger, eds., *Agnotology: The Making and Unmaking of Ignorance* (Palo Alto, CA: Stanford University Press, 2008).

34. Steven Shapin, *The Social History of Truth: Civility and Science in Seventeenth-Century England* (Chicago: University of Chicago Press, 1994).

35. Loraine Daston, "Baconian Facts, Academic Civility, and the Prehistory of Objectivity," in *Rethinking Objectivity*, ed. Allan Megill (Durham, NC: Duke University Press, 1994), 37–63; and "Strange Facts, Plain Facts, and the Texture of Scientific Experience in the Enlightenment," in *Proof and Persuasion: Essays on Authority, Objectivity and Evidence*, ed. Suzanne Marchand and Elizabeth Lunbeck (Turnhout, Belgium: Brepols, 1996), 42–59.

36. *Voltaire's Philosophical Dictionary: unabridged and unexpurgated* (Paris: E. R. DuMont, 1901 [1765 edition]), vol. 4, 326, and vol. 10, 130, respectively.

37. See the introductory essay in *The Craftsman*, ed. Caleb d'Anvers [pseud.], vol. 1 (December 5, 1726). "Craft" here means essentially craftiness.

38. Jürgen Habermas, *The Structural Transformation of the Public Sphere: An Inquiry into a Category of Bourgeois Society*, trans. Thomas Burger (Cambridge, MA: MIT Press, 1991 [1962]), 25. See too Jon Snyder, *Dissimulation and the Culture of Secrecy in Early Modern Europe* (Berkeley: University of California Press, 2009), chapter 4, which explains the centrality of dissimulation (knowing everything and revealing nothing) to *raison d'état* politics.

39. Thomas Paine, *Common Sense* (1776), in *Rights of Man, Common Sense, and Other Political Writings*, ed. Mark Philp (Oxford: Oxford University Press, 1995), 9.

40. See Robert Darnton, *The Forbidden Bestsellers of Prerevolutionary France* (New York: Norton, 1996); and Sophia Rosenfeld, "The Social Life of the Senses: A New Approach to Eighteenth-Century Politics and Public Life," in *A Cultural History of the Senses in the Age of Enlightenment,* ed. Anne C. Vila (London: Bloomsbury, 2016), 21–39. Specifically on the advent of new forms of publicity in eighteenth-century politics, see Katlyn Marie Carter, "Practicing Politics in the Revolutionary Atlantic World: Secrecy, Publicity and the Making of Modern Democracy" (PhD dissertation, Princeton University, 2017).

41. See Jay, *Virtues of Mendacity,* 7, on the American "dream of transparent politics" stemming from "a powerful legacy of ruthless Puritan self-examination and insistence on interpersonal transparency" derived from Calvinism, as well as Enlightenment values. See too Mark A. Noll, *America's God: From Jonathan Edwards to Abraham Lincoln* (New York: Oxford University Press, 2002) on the development of "Christian republicanism."

42. Hannah Arendt, *The Human Condition,* 2nd ed. (Chicago: University of Chicago Press, 1998 [1958]), 278; and "Truth and Politics," 232.

43. For normative debates on this question today, see Elkins and Norris, eds., *Truth and Democracy.*

44. On the exceptionalism of Spanish America, where the "uncertainty" of republicanism was accompanied in many cases with laws making Catholicism the exclusive state religion, see Gabriel Entin, "Catholic Republicanism: The Creation of the Spanish American Republics during Revolution," *Journal of the History of Ideas* 79, no. 1 (2018): 105–23.

45. See Martha Nussbaum, "Political Objectivity," *New Literary History* 32, no. 4 (Autumn 2001): 883–906.

46. Arendt, *The Human Condition,* 290; and "Truth and Politics," 246.

47. Thomas Jefferson, letter to George Wythe of August 13, 1786, cited in Robert A. Ferguson, *Reading the Early Republic* (Cambridge, MA: Harvard University Press, 2004), 285–86.

48. John Rawls, *A Theory of Justice* (Cambridge, MA: Harvard University Press, 1990 [1971]), 480. See too "The Idea of Public

Reason Revisited" (1997), in *Collected Papers,* ed. Samuel Freeman (Cambridge, MA: Harvard University Press, 1999), 579–80.

49. Sheila Jasanoff defines "serviceable truths" as "robust statements about the condition of the world, with enough buy-in from both science and society to serve as a basis for collective decisions," and in which we are, at least temporarily, collectively confident without being entirely certain; see "Back from the Brink: Truth and Trust in the Public Sphere," *Issues in Science and Technology* 33, no. 4 (summer 2017), 25–28.

50. Harry Frankfurt, *On Truth* (New York: Knopf, 2006), 66.

51. See Sophia Rosenfeld, *A Revolution in Language: The Problem of Signs in Late Eighteenth-Century France* (Palo Alto, CA: Stanford University Press, 2001); and in the American context, Kenneth Cmiel, *Democratic Eloquence: The Fight over Popular Speech in Nineteenth-Century America* (Berkeley: University of California Press, 1990), esp. 39–49.

52. See Frederick Schauer, *Free Speech: A Philosophical Inquiry* (Cambridge, UK: Cambridge University Press, 1982), 15–46; and Larry Alexander, *Is There a Right of Freedom of Expression?* (Cambridge, UK: Cambridge University Press, 2005), 128–30, specifically on free speech justifications that link the search for truth and the flourishing of democracy.

53. Benjamin Franklin, "Silence Dogood," *New England Currant* (July 9, 1722), cited in Richard D. Brown, *The Strength of a People: The Idea of an Informed Citizenry in America, 1650–1870* (Chapel Hill: University of North Carolina Press, 1996), 28–29, an important study of the early context for many of these questions.

54. Alexander Meiklejohn, *Free Speech and Its Relation to Self-Government* (New York: Harper, 1948).

55. James Madison, speech of November 1794, quoted in Saul Cornell, *The Other Founders: Anti-Federalism and the Dissenting Tradition in America, 1788–1828* (Chapel Hill: University of North Carolina Press, 1999), 199.

56. "An Appeal to the Inhabitants of Quebec" (October 26, 1774), cited in Brown, *Strength of a People,* 67.

57. See Carole Pateman and Charles Mills, *Contract and Domination* (Cambridge, UK: Polity, 2007) on how racial, ethnic, and gender exclusions are built into the very notion of a social contract on which democracy rests; and Michael Hanchard, *The Spectre of Race: How Discrimination Haunts Democracy* (Princeton, NJ: Princeton University Press, 2018).

58. See Christopher Bickerton and Carlo Invernizzi Accetti, "Populism and Technocracy," in *The Oxford Handbook of Populism*, ed. Cristóbal Rovira Kaltwasser, Paul Taggart, et al. (Oxford: Oxford University Press, 2017), 326–41.

59. For examples, see Daniel A. Bell, *The Chinese Model: Political Meritocracy and the Limits of Democracy* (Princeton, NJ: Princeton University Press, 2015); or Jason Brennan, *Against Democracy* (Princeton, NJ: Princeton University Press, 2016).

60. See chapter 3.

61. Maximilien Robespierre, "Rapport sur les principes de morale politique qui doivent guider la Convention Nationale dans l'Administration intérieure de la République" (February 5, 1794) in his *Discours et rapports à la Convention,* cited in John Dunn, *Democracy: A History* (Toronto: Penguin Canada, 2006), 118.

62. On the misuse of the term even before the inauguration of President Trump, see Margaret Sullivan, "It's Time to Retire the Tainted Term 'Fake News,'" *Washington Post,* January 8, 2017, https://www.washingtonpost.com/lifestyle/style/its-time-to-retire -the-tainted-term-fake-news/2017/01/06/a5a7516c-d375-11e6 -945a-76f69a399dd5_story.html?noredirect=on&utm_term= .947fc410cc4d. On its weaponization, see Lucia Graves, "How Trump Weaponized 'Fake News' for His Own Political Ends," *Pacific Standard,* February 26, 2018, https://psmag.com/social -justice/how-trump-weaponized-fake-news-for-his-own-political -ends. On his false claim to have coined the term in the first place, see Callum Borchers, "Trump Falsely Claims (Again) That He Coined the Term 'Fake News,'" *Washington Post,* October 26, 2017, https://www.washingtonpost.com/news/the-fix/wp/2017/10/26 /trump-falsely-claims-again-that-he-coined-the-term-fake-news/ ?utm_term=.43709aa54fd8.

Chapter 2

1. Immanuel Kant, "An Answer to the Question: What Is Enlightenment?" trans. James Schmidt, in *What Is Enlightenment? Eighteenth-Century Answers to Twentieth-Century Questions,* ed. James Schmidt (Berkeley: University of California Press, 1996), 58–59.

2. Marquis de Condorcet, *Sketch for a Historical Picture of the Progress of the Human Mind* (1795, posthum.), in *Selected Writings,* ed. Keith M. Baker (Indianapolis: Bobbs-Merrill, 1976), 261.

3. Voltaire, "L'Homme," *Dictionnaire philosophique* (1764), quoted in Peter Gay, *The Enlightenment: An Interpretation. The Science of Freedom,* rev. ed. (New York: Norton, 1996), 4.

4. Condorcet, *Selected Writings,* 255. In other writings, Kant also expresses the typical prejudices of his moment on race and gender and cognitive capacity; see, for example, his *Observations on the Feeling of the Beautiful and Sublime* (1764) on the difference between female and male "understanding" and how, when it comes to black people, differences are "as great in regard to mental capacities" as they are in terms of color.

5. See Harvey Chisick, *The Limits of Reform in the Enlightenment: Attitudes toward the Education of the Lower Classes in Eighteenth-Century France,* 2nd ed. (Princeton, NJ: Princeton University Press, 2014); and Harry C. Payne, *The Philosophes and the People* (New Haven, CT: Yale University Press, 1976).

6. Peter Burke, *A Social History of Knowledge: From Gutenberg to Diderot* (Cambridge, UK: Polity, 2000), 119.

7. Jorge Cañizares-Esguerra, *How to Write the History of the New World: Histories, Epistemologies, and Identities in the Eighteenth-Century Atlantic World* (Palo Alto, CA: Stanford University Press, 2001).

8. Burke, *A Social History of Knowledge,* esp. 120; similar processes happened, probably earlier, in other non-European imperial contexts, but these are beyond the scope of this book. Still, see Sebastian Conrad, "Enlightenment in Global History: A Historiographical Critique," *American Historical Review* 117, no. 4 (October 2012): 1007, on how Chinese and Islamic scholars also

formulated, in the course of the eighteenth century, notions of the possibility of the autonomous discovery of truth via experience and reason.

9. Kant, *What Is Enlightenment?* 59.

10. Kant, *What Is Enlightenment?* 60.

11. On honor and honesty as gentlemanly attributes, see Joanne B. Freeman, *Affairs of Honor: National Politics in the New Republic* (New Haven, CT: Yale University Press, 2002); and in the French context, Charles Walton, *Policing Public Opinion in the French Revolution: The Culture of Calumny and the Problem of Free Speech* (Oxford: Oxford University Press, 2009).

12. Alexander Addison, *Reports of Cases in the County Courts of the Fifth Circuit* (1800), cited in Geoffrey Stone, *Perilous Times: Free Speech in Wartime from the Sedition Act of 1798 to the War on Terror* (New York: Norton, 2004), 562, note 32.

13. Roger Sherman, comments from Madison's "Notes on the Debates of the Constitutional Convention" (May 1787), cited in Seth Cotlar, "Languages of Democracy in America from the Revolution to the Election of 1800," in *Reimagining Democracy in the Age of Revolutions: America, France, Britain, Ireland, 1750–1850,* ed. Joanna Innes and Mark Philp (Oxford: Oxford University Press, 2013), 18.

14. On suffrage in the early U.S. republic, see Alexander Keyssar, *The Right to Vote: The Contested History of Democracy in the United States* (New York: Basic Books, 2000); and Chilton Williamson, *American Suffrage: From Property to Democracy, 1760–1860* (Princeton, NJ: Princeton University Press, 1960).

15. "Violence of the majority faction" is Madison's phrasing from no. 10 in *The Federalist Papers* (1787–1789). It corresponds to what John Adams called at almost the same moment "the tyranny of the majority" (see the third volume of his *A Defence of the Constitution of the Government of the United States of America* of 1788), which became a central preoccupation in the thought of J. S. Mill and Alexis de Tocqueville in the nineteenth century.

16. Burke, *A Social History of Knowledge,* 13 (on Richelieu); and Daniel Roche, *Les Républicains des lettres: gens de culture et Lumières au XVIIIe siècle* (Paris: Fayard, 1988), 168 (on D'Alembert).

17. See Sophia Rosenfeld, "Benjamin Rush's Common Sense," *Early American Studies* 15, no. 2 (Spring 2017): 252–73. On early modern efforts to develop formal training in politics, see Joseph Klaits, "Men of Letters and Political Reform in France at the End of the Reign of Louis XIV: The Founding of the Académie Politique," *Journal of Modern History* 43, no. 4 (December 1971): 577–97; and Peter Burke, *A Social History of Knowledge II: From the Encyclopédie to Wikipedia* (Cambridge, UK: Polity, 2012), 120, on the study of *Polizeiwissenschaft* in eighteenth-century German universities.

18. Thomas Jefferson, *Notes on the State of Virginia* (New York: Penguin, 1999 [1784]), 155.

19. See "A Bill for the More General Diffusion of Knowledge" (1779), in *Papers of Thomas Jefferson, vol. 2: 1777–18 June 1779*, ed. Julian P. Boyd (Princeton, NJ: Princeton University Press, 1950), 526–35; and Brown, *The Strength of a People*, 75–77. For the critique, see Luke Mayville, *John Adams and the Fear of American Oligarchy* (Princeton, NJ: Princeton University Press, 2016).

20. Johan N. Neem, *Democracy's Schools: The Rise of Public Education in America* (Baltimore: Johns Hopkins University Press, 2017), 26–30.

21. Richard Hofstadter, *Anti-Intellectualism in American Life* (New York: Knopf, 1963), esp. chapter 7.

22. Stone, *Perilous Times,* 34. On the highly partisan nature of the press in this era, see too Jeffrey L. Pasley, *"The Tyranny of Printers": Newspaper Politics in the Early American Republic* (Charlottesville: University of Virginia Press, 2001); and Marcus Daniel, *Scandal and Civility: Journalism and the Birth of American Democracy* (Oxford: Oxford University Press, 2010).

23. Addison writing in *Greenleaf's New Daily Advertiser* (February 21, 1799), cited in John C. Miller, *The Federalist Era, 1789–1801* (New York: Harper, 1960), 232.

24. Letter from Thomas Jefferson to Walter Jones, January 2, 1814, cited in Brown, *Strength of a People,* 88.

25. Neem, *Democracy's Schools,* 100.

26. On efforts to establish a less democratic form of republicanism after the Terror, see Andrew Jainchill, *Reimagining Politics after the Terror: The Republican Origins of French Liberalism* (Ithaca,

NY: Cornell University Press, 2008); and Bronislaw Baczko, *Ending the Terror: The French Revolution after Robespierre,* trans. Michael Petheram (Cambridge, UK: Cambridge University Press, 1994). On Napoleon's relationship to these efforts, see Louis Bergeron, *France under Napoleon,* trans. R. R. Palmer (Princeton, NJ: Princeton University Press, 1981).

27. This paragraph is drawn from Rosenfeld, *A Revolution in Language,* chapter 5; see 185, 188, 204 for quotes. On the White House's recent turn away from the use of stenography to record conversations, see Jason Breslow, "Ex-White House Stenographer: With No Official Transcript, Trump Can Muddle the Truth," NPR, July 23, 2018, https://www.npr.org/2018/07/23/630643035/ex -white-house-stenographer-with-no-official-transcript-trump-can -muddle-the-tru.

28. Condorcet, *Selected Writings,* 266.

29. See Aurelian Craiutu, "Faces of Moderation: Mme de Staël Politics during the Directory," *Jus Politicum* no. 6 (2008). The comparison with Jefferson is drawn from Mayville, *John Adams,* 64–65. On the centrality of the idea of a "natural aristocracy" to early modern republicanism, from James Harrington to Jefferson, see Jainchill, *Reimagining Politics,* 129–36.

30. See Burke, *A Social History of Knowledge II,* 222.

31. Robert Justin Goldstein, ed., *The War for the Public Mind: Political Censorship in Nineteenth-Century Europe* (Westport, CT: Praeger, 2000), 29.

32. See Toon Kerkhoff, Ronald Kroeze, and Pieter Wagenaar, "Corruption and the Rise of Modern Politics in Europe in the Eighteenth and Nineteenth Centuries: A Comparison Between France, the Netherlands, Germany and England," *Journal of Modern European History* 11, no. 1 (2013): 19–30.

33. Peter Dear, "Mysteries of State, Mysteries of Nature: Authority, Knowledge and Expertise in the Seventeenth Century," in *States of Knowledge: The Co-Production of Science and the Social Order,* ed. Sheila Jasanoff (London: Routledge, 2004), 206–24, explains the origins of the term *expert,* of which the *Oxford English Dictionary* finds the first use in 1825, and its relationship to experience. On expertise and democracy, see too Thomas L. Haskell, ed.,

The Authority of Experts: Studies in History and Theory (Bloomington: Indiana University Press, 1984); Michael Schudson, "The Trouble with Experts—and Why Democracies Need Them," *Theory and Society* 35, nos. 5–6 (December 2006): 491–506; and Alfred Moore, *Critical Elitism: Deliberation, Democracy, and the Problem of Expertise* (Cambridge, UK: Cambridge University Press, 2017).

34. The myth first appeared in Federalist Mason Locke Weems's popular biography *The Life of Washington the Great: Enriched with a Number of Very Curious Anecdotes, Perfectly in Character, and Equally Honorable to Himself, and Exemplary to His Young Countrymen* (1806) and was furthered by its inclusion in nineteenth-century McGuffey readers; see Ed Lengel, *Inventing George Washington: America's Founder in Myth and Memory* (New York: HarperCollins, 2010).

35. On America's orientation toward policy-making—understood as collective problem-solving, backed by expertise—albeit within a framework of substantial constitutional restraints and with considerable opposition from the beginning, see Karen Orren and Stephen Skowronek, *The Policy State: An American Predicament* (Cambridge, MA: Harvard University Press, 2017).

36. On the history of the U.S. census, see James H. Cassedy, *Demography in Early America: Beginnings of the Statistical Mind, 1600–1800* (Cambridge, MA: Harvard University Press, 1969); William Alonso and Paul Starr, eds., *The Politics of Numbers* (Albany, NY: Russell Sage Foundation, 1987); and Margo J. Anderson, *The American Census: A Social History*, 2nd ed. (New Haven, CT: Yale University Press, 2015).

37. See Patricia Cline Cohen, *A Calculating People: The Spread of Numeracy in Early America* (Chicago: University of Chicago Press, 1982). On the history of statistics as a form of knowledge, see too Theodore M. Porter, *The Rise of Statistical Thinking, 1820–1900* (Princeton, NJ: Princeton University Press, 1986); Ian Hacking, *The Taming of Chance* (Cambridge, UK: Cambridge University Press, 1990); Alan Desrosières, *The Politics of Large Numbers: A History of Statistical Reasoning*, trans. Camille Naish (Cambridge, MA: Harvard University Press, 1998); and Burke, *A Social History of Knowledge II*, 65–68, 71, 124–25, 143, 233.

38. Anderson, *The American Census*, 23.

39. Gordon Wood, *The Radicalism of the American Revolution* (New York: Vintage, 1993), 360–61.

40. "Representing things as they really are" is Richard Rorty's phrase (see *Philosophy and the Mirror of Nature*, 1979), which is quoted in Megill, ed., *Rethinking Objectivity*. It echoes John Dewey, who described "the prima facie meaning of truth" as "seeing things as they are and reporting them as they are seen"; see "The Problem of Truth" (1911), in *The Political Writings*, ed. Debra Morris and Ian Shapiro (Indianapolis, IN: Hackett, 1993), 10.

41. Theodore Porter, *Trust in Numbers: The Pursuit of Objectivity in Science and Public Life* (Princeton, NJ: Princeton University Press, 1995), 90; see esp. parts II and III.

42. In the first chapter of the *Communist Manifesto* (1848), Karl Marx and Friedrich Engels famously claimed that one of the hallmarks of the bourgeoisie in the era of industrial capitalism was a qualitative understanding of the world, or the replacement of religion, sentimentality, and other ideologies with "the icy waters of egotistical calculation"; see *The Marx-Engels Reader*, ed. Robert C. Tucker (New York: Norton, 1978), 475. Marx would, though, go on to employ statistical methods himself in later work, including *Capital* (1867).

43. On the rise of professionals, with particular claims to knowledge, see especially Kenneth Alder, "Engineers Become Professionals, or How Meritocracy Made Knowledge Objective," in *The Sciences in Enlightenment Europe*, ed. William Clark et al. (Chicago: University of Chicago Press, 1999); and Peter Novick, *That Noble Dream: The "Objectivity Question" and the American Historical Profession* (Cambridge, UK: Cambridge University Press, 1988), as well as a large literature on the rise of professionals in a variety of different national political contexts.

44. Anderson, *The American Census*, 56–57.

45. Allan Megill, in the introduction to *Rethinking Objectivity*, distinguishes "disciplinary objectivity," based on the intersubjective consensus of the practitioners of a discipline, from "procedural objectivity," based on the impersonal methods and rules employed in the business of investigation; but here they clearly overlap.

46. For example, C. A. Bayly, *Empire and Information: Intelligence Gathering and Social Communication in India, 1780–1870* (Cambridge, UK: Cambridge University Press, 1996), though Bayly stresses the role of indigenous people as well as British authorities in shaping knowledge in colonial India.

47. Charles A. Hale, *The Transformation of Liberalism in Late Nineteenth-Century Mexico* (Princeton, NJ: Princeton University Press, 1989), esp. chapter 4.

48. C. A. Bayly, *The Birth of the Modern World, 1780–1914* (Malden, MA: Blackwell, 2004), 308, 319.

49. Miriam Valverde, "What You Need to Know about the Census' Citizenship Question," *Politifact*, March 28, 2018, https://www.politifact.com/truth-o-meter/article/2018/mar/28/what-you-need-know-about-census-citizenship-questi/.

50. John Dewey, *Psychology and Philosophical Method* (1899), cited in James T. Kloppenberg, *Uncertain Victory: Social Democracy and Progressivism in European and American Thought, 1870–1920* (New York: Oxford University Press, 1986), 384, an essential study of the relationship between the epistemological and political visions of the Progressives. See too Robert B. Westbrook, *John Dewey and American Democracy* (Ithaca, NY: Cornell University Press, 1991); Leon Fink, *Progressive Intellectuals and the Dilemmas of Democratic Commitment* (Cambridge, MA: Harvard University Press, 1997); and Andrew Jewett, *Science, Democracy, and the American University from the Civil War to the Cold War* (Cambridge, UK: Cambridge University Press, 2012).

51. Dewey, *The Public and Its Problems* (Denver, CO: Alan Swallow, 1927), 209, 210.

52. Dewey, *The Public and Its Problems*, 208–9.

53. On the rise in both the United Kingdom and the United States of the modern welfare state in tandem with academic social-scientific research, see Dietrich Rueschemeyer and Theda Skocpol, eds., *States, Social Knowledge, and the Origins of Modern Social Policies* (Princeton, NJ: Princeton University Press, 1996; new ed. 2017).

54. Roy MacLeod, *Government and Expertise: Specialists, Administrators and Professionals, 1860–1919* (Cambridge, UK: Cambridge University Press, 1988), 20.

55. James K. Conant, *Wisconsin Politics and Government: America's Laboratory of Democracy* (Lincoln: University of Nebraska Press, 2006).

56. On the rise of the idea of facticity and then objectivity in news reporting, see Michael Shudson, *Discovering the News: A Social History of American Newspapers* (New York: Basic Books, 1978); and David T. Z. Mindich, *Just the Facts: How "Objectivity" Came to Define American Journalism* (New York: New York University Press, 1998).

57. This famous line comes from the conclusion of Ida B. Wells, *The Red Record: Tabulated Statistics and Alleged Causes of Lynching in the United States* (Chicago: Donohue and Henneberry, 1895).

58. Ken Alder, "To Tell the Truth: The Polygraph Exam and the Marketing of American Expertise," *Historical Reflections/Réflexions historiques* 24, no. 3 (Fall 1998): 487–525.

59. Martin J. Schiesl, *The Politics of Efficiency: Municipal Administration and Reform in America, 1800–1920* (Berkeley: University of California Press, 1977).

60. Anon., "City Managing as New Profession," *Independent*, December 14, 1914.

61. See Kloppenberg, *Uncertain Victory*, 270–74.

62. Max Weber, "Bureaucracy" (1922), in *From Max Weber: Essays in Sociology*, ed. H. H. Gerth and C. Wright Mills (New York: Oxford University Press, 1946), 196–244. See Kloppenberg, *Uncertain Victory*, 381–94; Peter Breiner, *Max Weber and Democratic Politics* (Ithaca, NY: Cornell University Press, 1996), esp. 132–39; and Jennifer M. Hudson, "The Bureaucratic Mentality in Democratic Theory and Contemporary Democracy," PhD dissertation, Columbia University, 2016.

63. Raymond Smock, "The Value of Federal History," *Federal History*, no. 5 (January 2013): 1–14.

64. See Nadia Hilliard, *The Accountability State: US Federal Inspectors General and the Pursuit of Democratic Integrity* (Lawrence: University Press of Kansas, 2017). The Inspector General Act dates from 1978.

65. Orren and Skowronek, *The Policy State*, 8.

66. Herrick Chapman, *France's Long Reconstruction: In Search of the Modern Republic* (Cambridge, MA: Harvard University Press, 2018) focuses on the role of experts and civilians alike in this process.

67. Emmanuel Macron, "Speech at the United States Congress" (transcript), April 25, 2018, Voltaire Network, http://www.voltairenet.org/article200927.html.

68. On technocratic governance, see Frank Fischer, *Technocracy and the Politics of Expertise* (Newberry Park, CA: Sage, 1990); and Jürgen Habermas, *The Lure of Technocracy*, trans. Ciaran Cronin (Cambridge, UK: Polity, 2015); though the term is a modern one, its roots go back to the nineteenth century and the thought of Saint-Simon and Comte, if not Bacon. See too Antoine Picon, "French Engineers and Social Thought, 18th–20th Centuries: An Archeology of Technocratic Ideals," *History and Technology* 23, no. 3 (2007): 197–208.

69. On the downsides of planning schemes, see James C. Scott, *Seeing Like a State: How Certain Schemes to Improve the Human Condition Have Failed* (New Haven, CT: Yale University Press, 1998).

70. Specifically on the role of experts in colonial "development" and "modernization" projects, see Frederick Cooper and Randall Packard, eds., *International Development and the Social Sciences: Essays on the History and Politics of Knowledge* (Berkeley: University of California Press, 1998); Timothy Mitchell, *Rule of Experts: Egypt, Techno-Politics, Modernity* (Berkeley: University of California Press, 2002); and, for an alternative point of view insofar as it also stresses Western scientific experts' role in undermining imperialism, Erik Linstrum, *Ruling Minds: Psychology in the British Empire* (Cambridge, MA: Harvard University Press, 2016).

71. Scott, *Seeing Like a State*, 225–27; but also Helen Tilley, *Africa as a Living Laboratory: Empire, Development and the Problem of Scientific Knowledge, 1870–1950* (Chicago: University of Chicago Press, 2011).

72. Kevin Featherstone, "Jean Monnet and the Democratic Deficit in the European Union," *Journal of Common Market Studies* 32, no. 2 (1994): 149–70; and Claudio M. Radaelli, *Technocracy in the European Union* (New York: Longman, 1999). For comparison,

see Patricio Silva, *In the Name of Reason: Technocrats and Politics in Chile* (University Park: Penn State University Press, 2009); and Eduardo Dargent, *Technocracy and Democracy in Latin America: The Experts Running Government* (New York: Cambridge University Press, 2015).

73. Dunn, *Democracy: A History,* 51.

74. See the nation-by-nation survey of recent European party politics in Jon Henley, Helena Bengtsson, and Caelainn Barr, "Across Europe, Distrust of Mainstream Political Parties Is on the Rise," *Guardian,* May 25, 2016, https://www.theguardian.com/world/2016/may/25/across-europe-distrust-of-mainstream-political-parties-is-on-the-rise. On the similarity of patterns in the United States and Europe, see Saskia Brechenmacher, "Comparing Democratic Distress in the US and Europe," Carnegie Foundation for Peace, June 21, 2018, https://carnegieendowment.org/2018/06/21/comparing-democratic-distress-in-united-states-and-europe-pub-76646.

75. On the complaints, which have been augmented by UKIP and Conservative leaders, but also the complexities of the question of the European Union's impact on fishermen in Scotland and England, see Kait Bolongardo, "Fishy Brexit Dilemma: Want Out of EU but Need the Market," *Politico,* May 18, 2018, https://www.politico.eu/article/brexit-scotland-fishing-industry-divide/; and John Lichfield, "Ukip Is Wrong: British Fishing Answers to Westminster not Brussels," *Guardian,* April 6, 2018, https://www.theguardian.com/commentisfree/2018/apr/06/ukip-british-fishing-westminster-brussels-brexit.

76. J. S. Mill introduced the term "pedantocracy" (as what we must avoid bureaucracy degenerating into) in *On Liberty* (1859); see *The Basic Writings of John Stuart Mill,* ed. J. B. Schneewind and Dale E. Miller (New York: Modern Library, 2002), 117. Patrick Deneen, in his hyperbolic critique of the pathologies of liberalism, insists we should think more broadly of a "cognitive elite" that he calls "liberalocracy"; see his "The Tragedy of Liberalism," *Hedgehog Review* 19, no. 3 (Fall 2017).

77. Deepa Naragan, "The Contribution of People's Participation: Evidence from 121 Rural Water Supply Projects," Environmentally

Sustainable Development Occasional Paper Series, no. 1, World Bank (Washington, D.C.: 1995), http://documents.worldbank.org /curated/en/750421468762366856/pdf/38294.pdf.

78. Arendt, "Lying in Politics," 35.

79. See Jacques Ellul, *Propaganda: The Formation of Men's Attitudes*, trans. Konrad Kellen and Jean Lerner (New York: Knopf, 1965 [1962]) for another effort of the same era to understand forms of lying particular to modern "technological society."

80. Ruchir Sharma, "When Forecasters Get It Wrong: Always," *New York Times*, December 31, 2017, https://www.nytimes.com /2017/12/30/opinion/sunday/when-forecasters-get-it-wrong -always.html.

81. Eric Lipton and Brooke Williams, "How Think Tanks Amplify Corporate America's Influence," *New York Times*, August 7, 2016, https://www.nytimes.com/2016/08/08/us/politics /think-tanks-research-and-corporate-lobbying.html.

82. Arendt, "Truth and Politics," 241.

Chapter 3

1. On this myth, see Edmund S. Morgan, *Inventing the People: The Rise of Popular Sovereignty in England and America* (New York: Norton, 1988); and Pierre Rosanvallon, *Le Peuple introuvable: Histoire de la représentation démocratique en France* (Paris: Gallimard, 1998).

2. See Bayly, *The Birth of the Modern World*, 107, 166–67, on how "the people," post-1789, also became a global template for resistance.

3. James Burgh, *Crito, or Essays on Various Subjects* (1766), cited in Brown, *Strength of a People*, 47.

4. John Stuart Mill, *Considerations on Representative Government* (1861), ed. Geraint Williams (London: Dent, 1993), 225–26. The comment about "barbarians" who have not yet reached intellectual maturity still requiring "despotism" to keep them in line comes from Mill, *On Liberty*; see *The Basic Writings of John Stuart Mill*, 12.

5. On inverse inegalitarianism, see Jack Hayward, "The Populist Challenge to Elitist Democracy in Europe," in *Elitism, Populism, and European Politics*, ed. Hayward (New York: Oxford University Press, 1996), who borrows the term from Edward Shils, *The Torment of Secrecy: The Background and Consequences of American Security Policies* (1956). The seeds of this notion could be said to go back to Michel de Montaigne's essay "On Cannibals," published first in his *Essais* (1580).

6. Olympe de Gouges, *Le Bon sens François, ou l'Apologie des vrais nobles dédiée aux Jacobins* (April 1792), in *Olympe de Gouges: Ecrits politiques, 1792–1793*, ed. Olivier Blanc (Paris: Côté-femmes, 1993), 75.

7. See, for example, [C. D. Lacoste-Mezières], *Lettre d'un vieillard de bon sens* (Marseille, c. 1790); Plain Farmer of Huntingdonshire, *Two Letters on the Corn Laws . . .* (Oundle [England], 1827); or "One of the People," *Pennsylvania Evening Post*, November 23, 1776.

8. On faith in the wisdom of crowds now, see Benjamin I. Page and Robert Y. Shapiro, *The Rational Public: Fifty Years of Trends in American Policy Preferences* (Chicago: University of Chicago Press, 1992); Jeremy Waldron, "The Wisdom of the Multitude: Some Reflections on Book 3, Chapter 11 of Aristotle's Politics," *Political Theory* 23, no. 4 (November 1995): 563–84; and, in a more popular vein, James Surowiecki, *The Wisdom of Crowds: Why the Many Are Smarter than the Few and How Collective Wisdom Shapes Business, Economies, Societies and Nations* (New York: Doubleday, 2004); and Cass Sunstein, *Infotopia: How Many Minds Produce Knowledge* (Oxford: Oxford University Press, 2006).

9. On the defense of democracy on epistemic grounds, see Joshua Cohen, "An Epistemic Conception of Democracy," *Ethics* 97, no. 1 (October 1986): 26–38; David Estlund, "Making Truth Safe for Democracy," in *The Idea of Democracy*, ed. David Copp, Jean Hampton, et al. (Cambridge, UK: Cambridge University Press, 1993), 71–100; Elizabeth Anderson, "The Epistemology of Democracy," *Episteme* 3, no. 1–2 (2006): 8–22; and Hélène Landemore, *Democratic Reason: Politics, Collective Intelligence, and the*

Rule of the Many (Princeton, NJ: Princeton University Press, 2013), which gives this argument a prehistory, from the ancients through Spinoza, Rousseau, Condorcet, Mill, Dewey, and Hayek.

10. On the logic of juries, see Leonard Levy, *The Palladium of Justice: Origins of Trial by Jury* (Chicago: I. R. Dee, 1999); and James Q. Whitman, *The Origins of Reasonable Doubt: Theological Roots of the Criminal Trial* (New Haven, CT: Yale University Press, 2008).

11. Thomas Andrew Green, *Verdict According to Conscience: Perspectives on the English Criminal Trial Jury, 1200–1800* (Chicago: University of Chicago Press, 1985), 343.

12. See the arguments of Leonarde Keeler, one of the inventors of the polygraph and the author of "The Jury System Should be Abolished" (1930), in Alder, "To Tell the Truth."

13. Serena Ferente et al., eds., *Cultures of Voting in Pre-Modern Europe* (London: Routledge, 2018); and Olivier Christin, *Vox Populi: Une histoire du vote avant le suffrage universel* (Paris: Seuil, 2014).

14. See George McKenna, introduction to *American Populism* (New York: Putnam, 1974).

15. Key theoretical accounts of populism in relation to democracy include Margaret Canovan, *Populism* (New York: Harcourt Brace Jovanovich, 1981) and *The People* (Cambridge, UK: Polity Press, 2005); Pierre-André Taguieff, *L'Illusion populiste: De l'archaïque au médiatique* (Paris: Berg, 2002) and ed., *Le Retour de populisme: Un défi pour les démocraties européennes* (Paris: Universalis, 2004); Francisco Panizza, ed., *Populism and the Mirror of Democracy* (London: Verso, 2005); Ernesto Laclau, *On Populist Reason* (London: Verso, 2005); Pierre Rosanvallon, "Penser le populisme," *La Vie des Idées*, January 27, 2011, http://www.laviedesidees.fr/Penser-le-populisme.html; and Jan-Werner Müller, *What Is Populism?* (Philadelphia: University of Pennsylvania Press, 2016).

16. On the epistemological foundations of populism, see Sophia Rosenfeld, *Common Sense: A Political History* (Cambridge, MA: Harvard University Press, 2011); and Thomas Dumm, *A Politics of the Ordinary* (New York: New York University Press, 1999).

17. See Mark Fenster, *Conspiracy Theories: Secrecy and Power in American Culture* (Minneapolis: University of Minnesota Press,

2008 [1999]) on the transformative role of the truth-seeker within conspiracy theories.

18. This argument is explained at length in Rosenfeld, *Common Sense: A Political History*, esp. introduction and chapters 1–3.

19. On this title, variably *L'Espion anglais* and *L'Observateur anglais*, see Rosenfeld, "The Social Life of the Senses." More generally on these sorts of periodicals, known as *chroniques scandaleuses*, see Darnton, *The Forbidden Best-Sellers of Pre-Revolutionary France*, 79–82.

20. Richard Hofstadter, *The Paranoid Style in American Politics and Other Essays* (New York: Knopf, 1965); Gordon Wood, "Conspiracy and the Paranoid Style: Causality and Deceit in the Eighteenth Century," *William and Mary Quarterly* 39, no. 3 (July 1982): 401–44; Peter Campbell et al., eds., *Conspiracy in the French Revolution* (Manchester, UK: Manchester University Press, 2007); and Timothy Tackett, "Conspiracy Obsession in a Time of Revolution: French Elites and the Origins of the Terror, 1789–1792," *American Historical Review* 105, no. 3 (2000): 691–713.

21. Paine, *Common Sense* (1776), in *Rights of Man, Common Sense, and Other Political Writings*, 27.

22. Rosenfeld, *Common Sense*, chapter 4.

23. Amos Singletary (c. 1788), cited in Ronald Formisano, *For the People: American Populist Movements from the Revolution to the 1850s* (Chapel Hill: University of North Carolina Press, 2008), 35.

24. See Centinel, "X: To the People of Philadelphia" (e. 1788) and "XV: To the People of Philadelphia" (Feb. 20, 1788), *Independent Gazette*, in *The Complete Anti-Federalist*, ed. Herbert J. Storing (Chicago: University of Chicago Press, 1981), vol. 2, 183, 197.

25. Adams, "Letters to John Taylor," cited in Mayville, *John Adams*, 92.

26. See Samuel Williams, *Natural and Civil History of Vermont* (2nd ed., vol. 2, 1809), quoted in Wood, *Radicalism of the American Revolution*, 364.

27. Anon., *La Femme Patriote, ou le gros bon sens* (c. 1792).

28. For the text of the Law on Suspects, see "Extract from the Register of the Deliberations of the General Council of the Commune of Paris" (September 11, 1793), in *Readings in Western*

Civilization: 7, The Old Regime and the French Revolution, ed. Keith Baker (Chicago: University of Chicago Press, 1987), 338–39.

29. Edmund Burke, *Reflections on the Revolution in France,* ed. Frank M. Turner and Darrin McMahon (New Haven, CT: Yale University Press, 2003 [1790]), 110, 94, 96, 97.

30. Hofstadter, *Anti-Intellectualism in American Life,* 149, 147.

31. Patrick Joyce, *Visions of the People: Industrial England and the Question of Class, 1848–1914* (Cambridge, UK: Cambridge University Press, 1991).

32. Wood, *Radicalism of the American Revolution,* 361.

33. Elias Smith, *The Loving Kindness of God Displayed in the Triumph of Republicanism in America . . .* (1809), cited in Wood, *Radicalism of the American Revolution,* 332. See too Nathan Hatch, *The Democratization of American Christianity* (New Haven, CT: Yale University Press, 1989).

34. Letter in *Raleigh Register* (1829), cited in Brown, *Strength of a People,* 147.

35. Andrew W. Robertson, *The Language of Democracy: Political Rhetoric in the U.S. and Britain, 1790–1900* (Charlottesville: University of Virginia Press, 2005), 11, 71.

36. See Michael Kazin, *The Populist Persuasion: An American History,* rev. ed. (Ithaca, NY: Cornell University Press, 1998).

37. On the significance of an evangelical Christian notion of a moral sense to American political life, see Noll, *America's God.*

38. See the section entitled "The Attitude of the American Legal Profession and How It Acts as a Counterbalance to Democracy," in vol. I (1835), part II, chapter 8 ("What Moderates the Tyranny of the Majority in the United States") of Alexis de Tocqueville, *Democracy in America,* trans. Gerald E. Bevan (London: Penguin, 2003).

39. Ignatius Donnelly, "Omaha Platform" (July 1892), reproduced in *A Populist Reader: Selections from the Works of American Populist Leaders,* ed. George Brown Tindall (New York: Harper & Row, 1966), 92; Lloyd Rohler, *George Wallace: Conservative Populist* (Westport, CT: Praeger, 2004), 63; and Kazin, *The Populist Persuasion,* 240.

40. This song is mentioned in Alan Knight, "Populism and Neo-Populism in Latin America," *Journal of Latin American*

Studies 30, no. 2 (May 1998): 223–48, but the lyrics are translated differently.

41. Cited in George I. Blanksten, *Peron's Argentina* (Chicago: University of Chicago Press, 1953), 187. See too Federico Finchelstein, *The Ideological Origins of the Dirty War: Fascism, Populism and Dictatorship in Twentieth Century Argentina* (Oxford: Oxford University Press, 2014), 66–82.

42. Ronald Reagan, "Farewell Speech," January 11, 1989, http://www.presidency.ucsb.edu/ws/?pid=29650. On populist themes in the Reagan years, see too Kazin, *The Populist Persuasion*, 260–66, 270–71.

43. Molly Worthen, *Apostles of Reason: The Crisis of Authority in American Evangelicalism* (Oxford: Oxford University Press, 2014), esp. 251–53 on the 1980s (though she also points out that Baylor University, a Southern Baptist institution, started a program in Christian journalism as early as the 1960s).

44. See Sheila Jasanoff, *The Fifth Branch: Science Advisors as Policy Makers* (Cambridge, MA: Harvard University Press, 1990).

45. Alex Berezow and Hank Campbell, *Science Left Behind: Feel-Good Fallacies and the Rise of the Anti-Scientific Left* (New York: PublicAffairs, 2012).

46. Chris Mooney, *The Republican War on Science* (New York: Basic Books, 2005). For this empirical finding, see Gordon Gauchat, "Politicization of Science in the Public Sphere: A Study of Public Trust in the United States, 1974 to 2010," *American Sociological Review* 77, no. 2 (April 2012): 167–87, who demonstrates that declining support for science is not primarily a function of education levels but rather ideology.

47. Orren and Skowronek, *The Policy State*, 4.

48. See Hayward, "The Populist Challenge to Elitist Democracy in Europe." Chirac's speech is reported on in Jean-Louis Saux, "Le Retour au people de Jacques Chirac," *Le Monde*, January 21, 1995, who says this strategy goes back to De Gaulle. In the same issue of *Le Monde*, Bertrand Le Gendre, in "M. Chirac contre les 'experts,'" goes even further and identifies a multicentury tension in France between "technocratic jacobinism" and "anti-statist demagoguery."

49. Maryse Souchard et al., *Le Pen, les mots: Analyse d'un discours d'extrême droite* (Paris: Le monde éditions, 1997); and Taguieff, *L'Illusion*, 130.

50. See too, for this recent history, Cas Mudde, *Populist Radical Right Parties in Europe* (Cambridge, UK: Cambridge University Press, 2007); and Paul Taggart, "Populism in Western Europe," in *The Oxford Handbook of Populism*, 248–63.

51. Michael Deacon, "Michael Gove's Guide to Britain's Greatest Enemy . . . The Experts," *Telegraph*, June 10, 2016, https://www.telegraph.co.uk/news/2016/06/10/michael-goves-guide-to-britains-greatest-enemy-the-experts/.

52. For this economic argument, see Barry Eichengreen, *The Populist Temptation: Economic Grievance and Political Reaction in the Modern Era* (New York: Oxford University Press, 2018); and John Judis, *The Populist Explosion: How the Great Recession Transformed American and European Politics* (New York: Columbia Global Reports, 2016). It is important to note, though, that populism can be a reaction against neoliberalism and the triumph of market-based solutions without neoliberal economic policy becoming the real target at all.

53. On these policy proposals, see Linda Feldmann, "It's 'Common Sense'—Or Is It? The Politics of Obama's New Favorite Phrase," *Christian Science Monitor*, February 4, 2013, https://www.csmonitor.com/USA/Politics/2013/0204/It-s-common-sense-or-is-it-The-politics-of-Obama-s-new-favorite-phrase.

54. Bickerton and Accetti, "Populism and Technocracy," 328.

55. Judis, *The Populist Explosion*, 72.

56. Marc Fisher, "Donald Trump Doesn't Read Much. Being President Probably Wouldn't Change That," *Washington Post*, July 17, 2016, https://www.washingtonpost.com/politics/donald-trump-doesnt-read-much-being-president-probably-wouldnt-change-that/2016/07/17/d2ddf2bc-4932-11e6-90a8-fb84201e0645_story.html?noredirect=on&utm_term=.f6bc17c03ba9; and Ian Schwartz, "Trump: 'Within the First Minute' I'll Know Whether Kim Jong Un Is Serious," *RealClear Politics*, June 9, 2018, https://www.realclearpolitics.com/video/2018/06/09/trump_within_the_first_minute_know_kim_jong_un_serious.html.

57. Philip Bump, "How Trump's Wall Has Evolved (Despite His Denials That It Has)," *Washington Post,* January 18, 2018, https://www.washingtonpost.com/news/politics/wp/2018/01/18 /how-trumps-wall-has-evolved-despite-his-denials-that-it-has/ ?utm_term=.44720115ceb1.

58. Chauncey Devega, "Forget 'Civility': Take Donald Trump's Threats of Violence Seriously before It's Too Late," *Salon,* July 3, 2018, https://www.salon.com/2018/07/03/forget-civility-take -donald-trumps-threats-of-violence-seriously-before-its-too-late/.

59. Katie Rogers and Maggie Haberman, "Spotting CNN on a TV aboard Air Force One, Trump Rages against Reality," *New York Times,* July 24, 2018, https://www.nytimes.com/2018/07/24 /us/politics/trump-putin-cnn.html.

60. Arendt, "Truth and Politics," 257.

61. On the aims and impact of Czech dissident Václav Havel's "Power of the Powerless" of 1978, see "Living in Truth," *Economist,* December 31, 2011, https://www.economist.com/briefing/2011/12 /31/living-in-truth.

62. See the following studies and reports on the extent of internal division in the contemporary United States (http://www .pewresearch.org/fact-tank/2017/10/05/takeaways-on-americans -growing-partisan-divide-over-political-values/); in the United Kingdom (https://www.tandfonline.com/doi/full/10.1080/13501763 .2016.1225785); in Hungary (https://bbj.hu/analysis/majority-of -hungarians-see-deepened-social-divisions_148462); and in Turkey (http://tr.boell.org/de/2018/02/20/political-polarization-growing -turkish-society).

63. There are two bodies of recent literature here. One refers to a general crisis in popular reliance on vetted information, i.e., Thomas M. Nichols, *The Death of Expertise: The Campaign against Established Knowledge and Why It Matters* (New York: Oxford University Press, 2017) and Michael Specter, *Denialism: How Irrational Thinking Hinders Scientific Progress, Harms the Planet, and Threatens Our Lives* (New York: Penguin, 2009). The other is focused on the specific political crisis associated with the death of information under Trump, i.e., Michael Hayden, *The Assault on Intelligence: American National Security in an Age of Lies* (New York: Penguin,

2018) and Jennifer Kavanagh and Michael D. Rich, *Truth Decay: An Initial Exploration of the Diminishing Role of Facts and Analysis in American Public Life* (Santa Monica, CA: Rand, 2018). Needless to say, the authors of these tomes, whether Rand Corporation employees or former intelligence chiefs, often have a vested interest in their side of the story.

Chapter 4

1. See, for example, Paolo Rossi, *Logic and the Art of Memory: The Quest for a Universal Language,* trans. Stephen Clucas (Chicago: University of Chicago Press, 2000).

2. See, for example, Bert Hoffmann, "Civil Society 2.0? How The Internet Changes Society-State Relations in Authoritarian Regimes: The Case of Cuba," GIGA Working Papers, no. 156, January 2011, http://www.icnl.org/research/library/files/Cuba/civsoccuba.pdf. On the appeal in the 1990s of the idea of democracy promotion by digital means, see Evgeny Morozov, *The Net Delusion: The Dark Side of Internet Freedom* (New York: PublicAffairs, 2012), who offers a strong critique.

3. The classic account here is that of Elizabeth Eisenstein, *The Printing Press as an Agent of Change: Communications and Cultural Transformations in Early Modern Europe* (Cambridge, UK: Cambridge University Press, 1979).

4. There is, however, a substantial literature on the phenomenon of Trump himself, most of it highly critical, as in David Frum, *Trumpocracy: The Corruption of the American Republic* (New York: HarperCollins, 2018).

5. Rebecca Morin and David Cohen, "Giuliani: Truth Isn't Truth," *Politico,* August 19, 2018, https://www.politico.com/story/2018/08/19/giuliani-truth-todd-trump-788161; and Eric Bradner, "Conway: Trump White House Offered 'Alternative Facts' on Crowd Size," *Politico,* January 23, 2017, https://www.cnn.com/2017/01/22/politics/kellyanne-conway-alternative-facts/index.html.

6. The blame-postmodernism literature includes Michiko Kakutani, *The Death of Truth: Notes on Falsehood in the Age of*

Trump (New York: Tim Duggan Books, 2018); and Lee McIntyre, *Post-Truth* (Cambridge, MA: MIT Press, 2018), following influential earlier articles like Jeet Heer, "America's First Postmodern President," *New Republic,* July 18, 2017, https://newrepublic.com/article /143730/americas-first-postmodern-president; David Ernst, "Donald Trump Is the First President to Turn Postmodernism against Itself," *Federalist,* January 23, 2017, http://thefederalist.com/2017 /01/23/donald-trump-first-president-turn-postmodernism/; Marci Shore, "A Pre-History of Post-Truth, East and West," *Eurozine,* September 1, 2017, https://www.eurozine.com/a-pre-history-of-post -truth-east-and-west/; and, indeed, Carole Cadwalladr, "Daniel Dennett: 'I Begrudge Every Hour that I Have to Spend Worrying about Politics,'" *Guardian,* February 12, 2017, https://www .theguardian.com/science/2017/feb/12/daniel-dennett-politics -bacteria-bach-back-dawkins-trump-interview.

7. Frederick Schauer, "Facts and the First Amendment," *UCLA Law Review* 57, no. 4 (2010): 901, see https://www.uclalawreview .org/pdf/57-4-1.pdf.

8. Dziga Vertov, "The Factory of Facts [1928] and Other Writings," trans. Kevin O'Brian, *October 7* (Winter 1978): 109–28, see 128.

9. Cited in Blackburn, *Truth: A Guide,* 31.

10. Philip Rucker and Robert Costa, "Bannon Vows a Daily Fight for 'Deconstruction of the Administrative State,'" *Washington Post,* February 23, 2017, https://www.washingtonpost.com /politics/top-wh-strategist-vows-a-daily-fight-for-deconstruction -of-the-administrative-state/2017/02/23/03f6b8da-f9ea-11e6-bf01 -d47f8cf9b643_story.html?utm_term=.1540695562eb.

11. Richard Rorty, *Achieving Our Century* (Cambridge, MA: Harvard University Press, 1998), esp. 36, 97.

12. See David C. Barker, *Rushed to Judgment: Talk Radio, Persuasion, and American Political Behavior* (New York: Columbia University Press, 2002); Randy Bobbitt, *Us against Them: The Political Culture of Talk Radio* (Lanham, MD: Lexington Books, 2010); and, specifically on the epistemology of talk radio, in this case in the Canadian context, Paul Saurette and Shane Gunster,

"Ears Wide Shut: Epistemological Populism, Argutainment, and Canadian Conservative Talk Radio," *Canadian Journal of Political Science* 44, no. 1 (2011): 195–218.

13. See Gabriel Sherman, *The Loudest Voice in the Room: How the Brilliant, Bombastic Roger Ailes Built Fox News—and Divided a Country* (New York: Random House, 2014); and more generally on right-wing media, David Bell, "When the Farce *Is* Tragedy," *Dissent*, February 1, 2018, https://www.dissentmagazine.org/online_articles/trump-year-one-tragedy-farce-right-wing-media.

14. On the impact of left-wing satirical television, especially on the young, since the George W. Bush administration, see Amarnath Amarasingam, ed., *The Stewart/Colbert Effect: Essays on the Real Impacts of Fake News* (Jefferson, NC: McFarland, 2011); and S. Robert Lichter et al., *Politics Is a Joke!: How TV Comedians Are Remaking Political Life* (Boulder, CO: Westview Press, 2015).

15. See José van Dijck, *The Culture of Connectivity: A Critical History of Social Media* (New York: Oxford University Press, 2013). Facebook was founded in 2004, YouTube in 2005, and Twitter in 2006.

16. Robinson Meyer, "The Grim Conclusions of the Largest-Ever Study of Fake News," *Atlantic*, March 8, 2018, https://www.theatlantic.com/technology/archive/2018/03/largest-study-ever-fake-news-mit-twitter/555104/.

17. Jack Holmes, "Trump's Disgusting Retweets Suggest a Larger Problem Brewing," *Esquire*, November 29, 2017, https://www.esquire.com/news-politics/a13974149/trump-retweet-britain-first/.

18. Mike Isaac and Kevin Roose, "Disinformation Spreads on WhatsApp Ahead of Brazilian Election," *New York Times*, October 19, 2018, https://www.nytimes.com/2018/10/19/technology/whatsapp-brazil-presidential-election.html.

19. Harry Enten, "Fake Polls Are a Real Problem," *FiveThirtyEight*, August 22, 2017, https://fivethirtyeight.com/features/fake-polls-are-a-real-problem/.

20. Kevin Roose, "Here Come the Fake Videos, Too," *New York Times*, March 4, 2018, https://www.nytimes.com/2018/03/04/technology/fake-videos-deepfakes.html.

21. Cass R. Sunstein, *#Republic: Divided Democracy in the Age of Social Media* (Princeton, NJ: Princeton University Press, 2017); and Nadia Urbinati, *Democracy Disfigured: Opinion, Truth and the People* (Cambridge, MA: Harvard University Press, 2014).

22. Shashank Bengali and M. N. Parth, "Rumors of Child-Kidnapping Gangs and Other WhatsApp Hoaxes Are Getting People Killed in India," *Los Angeles Times,* May 20, 2018, http://www.latimes.com/world/asia/la-fg-india-whatsapp-2018-story.html#.

23. Steve Stecklow, "Why Facebook Is Losing the War on Hate Speech in Myanmar," *Reuters,* August 15, 1018, https://www.reuters.com/investigates/special-report/myanmar-facebook-hate/.

24. David Remnick, "Trump and the Enemies of the People," *New Yorker,* August 15, 2018, https://www.newyorker.com/news/daily-comment/trump-and-the-enemies-of-the-people; and Anon., "Trump to Players Who Kneel for the Anthem: 'Maybe You Shouldn't Be in the Country,'" *Guardian,* May 24, 2018, https://www.theguardian.com/sport/2018/may/24/donald-trump-lauds-nfl-anthem-policy.

25. Frederick Schauer, "Facts and the First Amendment."

26. Tim Wu, "Is the First Amendment Obsolete?" Knight First Amendment Institute, Columbia University, 2017, https://knightcolumbia.org/sites/default/files/content/Emerging%20Threats%20Tim%20Wu%20Is%20the%20First%20Amendment%20Obsolete.pdf.

27. Williams, *Truth and Truthfulness,* 215 modified.

28. Herbert Marcuse, "Repressive Tolerance," in Robert Paul Wolff, Barrington Moore Jr., and Marcuse, *A Critique of Pure Tolerance* (Boston: Beacon Press, 1969 [1965]), 95–137.

29. Theodore Roosevelt, "The Progressive Party Platform of 1912," *The American Presidency Project,* http://www.presidency.ucsb.edu/ws/index.php?pid=29617.

30. Arendt, *On Revolution* (New York: Viking, 1963), 96–101, and "Lying in Politics."

31. Serge Schmemann, "Arseny Roginsky, a Champion of Truth," *New York Times,* December 31, 2017, https://www.nytimes.com/2017/12/31/opinion/arseny-roginsky-champion-of-truth.html.

32. Chimamanda Ngozi Adichie, "Now Is the Time to Talk about What We Are Actually Talking About," *New Yorker,* December 2, 2016, https://www.newyorker.com/culture/cultural-comment/now-is-the-time-to-talk-about-what-we-are-actually-talking-about.

33. On the bullshit detector, see Mario Manlupig Jr., "Bullshit Detector Pins Down Fake News, False Claims in Real Time," *International Business Times,* August 10, 2017, http://www.ibtimes.sg/bullshit-detector-pins-down-fake-news-false-claims-real-time-13792; and S. Coleman, "The Elusiveness of Political Truth: From the Conceit of Objectivity to Intersubjective Judgment," *European Journal of Communication* 32, no. 2 (2018): 157–71.

34. David Cole, "Why We Must Still Defend Free Speech," *New York Review of Books,* September 28, 2017, https://www.nybooks.com/articles/2017/09/28/why-we-must-still-defend-free-speech/.

35. See *Buckly v. Valeo* 424 U.S. 1, 48-49 (1976).

36. Karen Zraick, "Mark Zuckerberg Seeks to Clarify Remarks about Holocaust Deniers after Outcry," *New York Times,* July 18, 2018, https://www.nytimes.com/2018/07/18/technology/mark-zuckerberg-facebook-holocaust-denial.html.

37. Tim Wu, "Is the First Amendment Obsolete?"

38. Adam Nossiter, "Macron Pushes Bill Aimed at 'Fake News' as Critics Warn of Dangers," *New York Times,* June 6, 2018, https://www.nytimes.com/2018/06/06/world/europe/macron-france-fake-news.html.

39. Polling data after the hearings showed that "Republicans and Democrats hold [or at least tell pollsters that they hold] starkly divergent views of whether his [Kavanaugh's] testimony to senators was credible"; see Alan Fram, "Just 1 in 4 Thinks Kavanaugh Told Entire Truth, Survey Says," *Boston Globe,* October 20, 2018, https://www.bostonglobe.com/news/nation/2018/10/19/just-thinks-kavanaugh-told-entire-truth-survey-says/MsNLKRIX2sLxOxflbiptAK/story.html.

40. W. Bradley Wendel, "Truthfulness as an Ethical Form of Life," Cornell Legal Studies Research Paper no. 17-48, 2017, https://papers.ssrn.com/sol3/papers.cfm?abstract_id=3072303.

41. See the new self-help literature on this front, which is generally marketed as psychology/business and economics, i.e., Daniel Levitin, *Weaponized Lies: How to Think Critically in the Post-Truth Era* (New York: Dutton, 2016); or, for a British example, Evan Davis, *Post-Truth: Why We Have Reached Peak Bullshit and What We Can Do About It* (London: Little, Brown, 2017).

42. See Greg Grandin and Thomas Miller Klubock, eds., "Truth Commissions: State Terror, History, and Memory," a special issue of *Radical History Review* 97 (2007).

43. Vanessa Williamson, "New Data Show that Police Violence Predicts Black Lives Matter Protests," Brookings Institution, May 17, 2018, https://www.brookings.edu/blog/fixgov/2018/05/17/new-data-show-that-police-violence-predicts-black-lives-matter-protests/.

44. Nicholas St. Fleur, "Scientists, Feeling under Siege, March against Trump Policies," *New York Times,* April 22, 2017, https://www.nytimes.com/2017/04/22/science/march-for-science.html and www.marchforscience.com.

45. Shruti Kapila, "Gandhi before Mahatma: The Foundations of Political Truth," *Public Culture* 23, no. 2 (2011): 431–48. The idea of knowledge as emancipatory when it results in one being newly able to see through the objective social world is also important to the European critical theory tradition.

46. Rosanvallon, "Penser le populisme."

47. See Wendy Brown, *Undoing the Demos: Neoliberalism's Stealth Revolution* (Cambridge, MA: MIT Press, 2015), 202, on whether democracy is really worth saving. Here she worries too about a "generalized collapse of faith in the powers of knowledge, reason, and will for the deliberative making and tending of our common existence" (221). But she appears to be less convinced of the centrality of truth to democracy in her 2012 contribution to Elkins and Norris, eds., *Truth and Democracy.*

Acknowledgments

This book was not road tested in all the usual ways. It benefited from no drafts of grant applications, invitations to speak, or dry-run articles. All the more reason I'm so grateful to Damon Linker at University of Pennsylvania Press for shepherding this project from idea to conclusion; to Francis Russo for extraordinary research assistance along the way; and to a small group of very smart, knowledgeable friends for conversations and expert readings that have really shaped what appears on these pages. All mistakes, omissions, and infelicities are, of course, my own, but there would be a lot more without their generous engagement with my words and ideas. That holds especially true—and this I say with certainty—for my family. As always, my biggest thanks go to those closest at hand, meaning Affrons and Rosenfelds.

CPSIA information can be obtained
at www.ICGtesting.com
Printed in the USA
LVHW092320091218
599858LV00001B/1/P